UNEMPLOYMENT, INFLATION AND NEW
MACROECONOMIC POLICY

By the same author

AUSTRALIA AND THE WORLD ECONOMY
BILLION DOLLAR QUESTIONS: Economic Issues for Australia in the 1970s
BRITAIN AND AUSTRALIA: Economic Relationships in the 1950s
CONTEMPORARY MACROECONOMICS (*co-author*)
CRISIS-POINT IN AUSTRALIAN ECONOMIC POLICY?
INTERNATIONAL POLICY FOR THE WORLD ECONOMY
MACRO-ECONOMIC POLICY: a Comparative Study (*co-author and editor*)
MACROECONOMIC POLICY IN AUSTRALIA
STERLING AND REGIONAL PAYMENTS SYSTEMS
THE AUSTRALIAN ECONOMY (*co-author*)
THE BANKS AND THE CAPITAL MARKET (*co-author*)
THE MACROECONOMIC MIX TO STOP STAGFLATION
THE PATTERN OF AUSTRALIA'S TRADE AND PAYMENTS
THE STERLING AREA, THE COMMONWEALTH AND WORLD ECONOMIC GROWTH

UNEMPLOYMENT, INFLATION AND NEW MACROECONOMIC POLICY

J. O. N. Perkins
Professor of Economics
University of Melbourne

© J. O. N. Perkins 1982

All rights reserved. No part of this publication may be reproduced or transmitted, in any form or by any means, without permission

First published 1982 by
THE MACMILLAN PRESS LTD
*London and Basingstoke
Companies and representatives
throughout the world*

ISBN 978-0-333-32116-4   ISBN 978-1-349-16784-5 (eBook)
DOI 10.1007/978-1-349-16784-5

The paperback edition of this book is sold subject to the condition that it shall not, by way of trade or otherwise, be lent, resold, hired out, or otherwise circulated without the publisher's prior consent, in any form of binding or cover other than that in which it is published and without a similar condition including this condition being imposed on the subsequent purchaser

To my colleagues at the University of Melbourne – for suffering so stoically and for so long their exposure to my ideas about the macroeconomic mix; and for their role in formulating and polishing these ideas

Contents

	Preface	ix
	Outline of the Basic Argument	xi
1	Introduction and Summary	1
2	Current Macroeconomic Problems and Policies	5
3	The Basic Proposals	23
4	Balance of Payments Aspects	53
5	The Mix, the Budget and the National Debt	68
6	Resource Allocation Policy and Macroeconomic Policy	90
7	Criticisms, Complications and Conclusions	108
	Notes and References	129
	Bibliography	132
	Index	134

Preface

This book is concerned with the crucial macroeconomic policy issue in the world economy at the start of the 1980s; namely, how to reduce both unemployment and inflation at the same time.

It is probably influenced disproportionately by the writer's interest in the economies of Britain (where he was born and educated, and had his first job – as a journalist) and Australia (where he has spent most of his working life – as an academic). But it has been influenced also by many helpful discussions on macroeconomic issues of common interest, with both official and academic economists in the USA and Canada, during visits in 1976 and 1980, and in Scandinavia (especially during a visit in 1980) and some other parts of Europe in 1976 and on several visits to the OECD and the IMF. In particular, the hospitality of the London School of Economics is gratefully acknowledged during several months in 1980–81, and during briefer visits in 1978 and 1979. The Institute of International Economic Studies in Stockholm provided kind and helpful hospitality on visits there in 1976 and 1980; and stimulus is acknowledged from very helpful seminars there, and at Aberdeen, Cambridge, Dundee, Manchester, Stirling, Strathclyde and at the London School of Economics as well as from various sessions at the University of Oklahoma, where Kirker Stephens made me very welcome and proved to have more ideas in common with mine on these issues than anyone else I have met. I have also received constant stimulus over the years from my colleagues at Melbourne, especially Ian McDonald.

The book *The Macroeconomic Mix to Stop Stagflation* contains a fuller exposition of the ideas underlying the basic policy proposals in the present book. These basic ideas are therefore merely summarised here (in Chapter 3). The present book consists mainly of developments and extensions of these basic ideas, together with discussion of comments on them (made by reviewers of the previous book, and by various participants in seminars and in private conversations), as well as drawing upon events and experience in various countries over the three years or so since the previous book was written. It may be said that one purpose of the previous book (as evidenced by its dedication) was to try to reduce the risk of the country of the author's birth from sliding down the slippery slopes of stagflationary policies that had been adopted in the second half of the 1970s by the government of the country of his adoption. With the additional evidence now available of the deficiencies of such policies, the time seems overripe for rethinking the future of macroeconomic policy in the light of the clear failures of the approach adopted in so many countries in the later 1970s and the beginning of the 1980s.

My thanks to my colleagues, Duncan Ironmonger, Bob Jones, Neville Norman, Sam Ouliaris, Alan Powell, Phyllis Rosendale and Peter Sheehan as well as to Kirker Stephens, who all read drafts of parts of the manuscript, but of course bear no responsibility for remaining deficiencies.

Jenny Gibson and Anne Marsden provided admirable and efficient secretarial assistance.

Melbourne, May 1981   J.O.N.P.

Outline of the Basic Argument

1. The unemployment of the 1930s occurred in the context of stable or falling prices. In such a situation *either* monetary expansion, *or* government spending, *or* tax cuts could reduce unemployment without causing undue increases in the price level.
2. The unemployment of recent years has, however, been coupled with rapid inflation. It is thus necessary to ask what combinations of measures will reduce unemployment whilst doing most to check the upward pressure on prices. So long as some macroeconomic measures have more upward effect than others on the price level for a given effect in increasing employment, there is some reduction in the expansionary effect of the former type of measure which can be combined with some stimulus to demand through the latter to stop stagflation.
3. Expansionary monetary measures are the *most* inflationary, and tax cuts are the *least* inflationary types of stimulus to employment. Most types of government spending are more inflationary than tax cuts. The best remedy for stagflation is thus tax cuts coupled with relatively tight monetary policies. Unfortunately, during the 1970s tax rates were raised to high levels and monetary policies were far too inflationary. A reversal of these policies is essential in order to stop stagflation.
4. The toleration of high unemployment for the purpose of trying to stop inflation may or may not be successful – depending on the measures used to hold up unemployment. But it is unnecessary, and socially wasteful, to attempt to use it for this purpose, because an appropriate change in the mix of macroeconomic measures can do as much to bring down inflation without the need for the unemployment. The world is being forced – unnecessarily – to tolerate the waste and human cost of high unemployment largely because governments are misusing their macroeconomic instruments, keeping taxes too high and real post-tax interest rates generally too low.

1 Introduction and Summary

At the start of the 1980s the world economy is suffering from higher unemployment than at any time since the 1930s: it is also suffering from a very high rate of inflation. In contrast to past recessions, the level of unemployment is high largely as the intended result of government policies: for the view that any measures that would reduce the unemployment would inevitably make inflation worse has become the conventional wisdom in most countries. Of course, not all of the unemployment is due to these policies, but much of the unemployment that might have been attributed to other factors would have disappeared if sounder macroeconomic policies had been applied.

Governments have tried to reduce the rate of inflation by holding down the level of demand (in real terms). This method was appropriate for dealing with the form of inflation resulting from excess demand at full employment that characterised a good deal of the three preceding decades. But it is highly inappropriate for tackling the type of inflation at well below full employment that has been the problem during most of the past decade.

The basic argument of this book is that appropriately chosen policies that will reduce unemployment need not lead to higher rates of inflation – and can, indeed, reduce the rate of inflation.[1] It is true that a change in the level of unemployment may in itself affect the level of prices – in one direction or the other. But this is not a very useful guide to policy. For the impact on the price level of a given stimulus to employment depends on the method selected for reducing unemployment at least as much as on the change in unemployment itself.

Unfortunately, during the 1970s – when almost all countries began to suffer from simultaneous unemployment and inflation ('stagflation') governments have generally adopted a combination of macroeconomic measures – namely, higher levels of taxation and low or negative real post-tax returns to the holders of financial assets – that has held up the rate of inflation at any given level of unemployment.[2] An important part of the solution to the problem of stagflation is thus to reduce the general level of taxation and to sell 'honest' bonds – that is to say, ones that no longer penalise lenders for holding them.[3] This is not to argue that the only factors

2 Unemployment, Inflation and New Macroeconomic Policy

raising the rate of inflation during the 1970s have been high taxes and low real interest rates. But an important part of the solution to the sort of problems that occurred during the 1970s and early 1980s is to bring the setting of these instruments to something like that which prevailed in the 1960s, when the world's macroeconomic problems were far less than in the 1970s, and certainly did not include stagflation.

The high level of unemployment in the 1970s has also made governments inclined to increase protection for particular industries – usually among the less economic – from the competition of imports. This has reduced the world's economic welfare by reducing the scope for it to benefit by international trade; and, just as high unemployment has affected adversely mainly people who are among those least well placed to bear it, so the various forms of protection against imports have tended to impinge most sharply on the exports of the relatively poorer nations, and to hold down the living standards of the lower income groups in the richer countries, as the excluded goods are predominantly mass-produced manufactures that are bought principally by the lower income groups.

Moreover, the continued low level of economic growth in the richer countries tended to reduce the prices and volumes of primary exports of the poorer countries – for whom primary exports are generally the main source of export receipts. These effects on the distribution of world income (away from the relatively poor), both within the richer countries and within the world economy as a whole, are liable to lead to serious economic and political strains during the coming decades. Yet the liberalisation of world trade is essential if prices are to be kept down and living standards to rise at an acceptable rate. But it is obviously politically difficult to reduce or remove the protection that assists the weaker and least economic industries in the developed countries so long as unemployment is high. For the people working in such industries naturally fear that if they have to quit their present jobs they may not readily find other employment.

In other words, the failure to solve the macroeconomic problem of stagflation is making it harder to achieve a more economic allocation of resources within the rich countries, and also an allocation of resources between the rich and the poor countries that would be of greater benefit to all the countries concerned. At the same time, failure to reallocate the resources of manpower in the rich countries towards the sort of industries that are most economic for such countries raises the rate of inflation in those countries – and so makes governments more inclined to allow unemployment to remain high in the hope of thereby reducing inflation. This is indeed a vicious circle. The macroeconomic problems and the resource allocation problems need therefore to be tackled simultaneously. The present book is concerned mainly with the macroeconomic problems, but the interrelationships between these two main groups of policy issues will also be discussed.

The problem is intensified by the rapid rate of technological change occurring *in particular industries*. The rapid progress of electronics has greatly raised productivity in a number of forms of production. This naturally gives rise to concern among those employed in more labour-intensive forms of production in the industries most affected by these scientific developments, thus often leading to calls for 'make-work' remedies for unemployment – to slow down the rate of technological application, or to introduce mandatory shorter hours and early retirement. Yet productivity *generally* has not been rising rapidly; indeed, its rate of increase slowed down considerably during the 1970s; and to forgo the rise in living standards made possible by technological developments would further reduce the rise in productivity, and so hold down living standards and make it harder to restrain inflation. Certainly, the countries that are least prepared to make full use of these new technological possibilities are likely to have slower increases in their living standards, and more severe macroeconomic problems, than those that adapt well to the new range of technological possibilities. But reasonable solutions to these problems cannot be discussed without seeing them in their macroeconomic context; for unless the government of the country concerned is pursuing policies that will make it possible for people who have to change their jobs to be readily re-employed elsewhere, there is bound to be continued distrust of the new technological developments in many places.

There is much that the government of an individual country can do even by itself to cope with these problems. But it is certainly preferable that the appropriate policies to handle them should be concerted internationally. There are various international institutions and other international arrangements that could helpfully be modified to restore a high level of world economic growth without inflation. In particular, there are policies that could usefully be followed by the International Monetary Fund and by the European Economic Community that would facilitate the solving of the problem of stagflation.

On the other hand, some people fear some of the consequences that they expect to result from a higher rate of economic growth if full employment were restored, and especially the strains that high growth rates may impose on the finite resources of the planet. But, on examination, these turn out to be fears of the consequences of *particular forms of growth*; and the adverse consequences that some observers fear are not, in any case, appropriately avoided by tolerating inflation and high unemployment – which impose the costs and sacrifices of the slow growth upon many of those least able to bear it. Certainly, the particular pattern of consumption and production is at least as important a determinant of the rate at which the planet uses its resources as is the overall rate of economic growth. But the level of economic activity is also an important influence upon the rate of new discoveries of scarce resources, and of ways to make the best use of them. Stagflation not only holds back the demands upon those resources at present available, but also reduces the incentive for people to discover new resources and better ways of using old ones. Furthermore, the pricing policies pursued by governments are an important element in determining the rate at which scarce resources are depleted. Any government that fails to ensure that its consumers pay the full world price for oil – the price reflecting its relative scarcity – is in no position to argue that output and employment should be held down in order to economise in the use of oil and other scarce resources. Yet governments in the later 1970s and early 1980s were resorting to unemployment partly in order to offset the upward effect on their countries' demand for oil that results from holding down the prices paid for oil by consumers.

This is one of many matters on which it is difficult to secure the adoption of sensible policies unless there is widespread public understanding of the economic issues and of what are the general lines of appropriate solutions to them. One important step is to secure a consensus among economic policy-makers as to what is desirable; but the possibility of applying rational economic policies (at least in democratic countries) depends in the last resort also on how far the policies are understood and accepted by public opinion.

Yet there are grounds for hope in that the basic situation is one in which there is widespread underutilisation of resources. For this means that there is – in principle – a 'free lunch' available, in the special sense that if the people who are able and willing to work can be brought into productive use, living standards everywhere can rise. Rational economic policies do not call, therefore, for material sacrifices on the part of people generally, though they are likely to call for changes in particular policies from which particular vested interests benefit (or think they benefit). Certainly, the presumption that only medicine that tastes nasty is good for you is as wide of the mark as the opposite fallacy that there is an easy way out that treads on no-one's toes. Moralistic biases in either of these directions are not, therefore, conducive to objective discussion of the issues. It is true that one task of political leadership is to override misguided and selfish objections where they stand in the way of sound policies; but more harm than good will be done by adopting the attitude that the appropriate measures must always cause pain if they are to be successful.

2 Current Macroeconomic Problems and Policies

The combination of high unemployment and high inflation that became established in the later 1970s began to appear in the later 1960s, when inflation started to increase. During the period of higher inflation in the first half of the 1970s, unemployment rates also remained well above the levels that had generally prevailed since World War Two. Table 2.1 illustrates the deterioration of the macroeconomic situation in the OECD countries (the developed countries of Europe and North America, together with Japan, Australia and New Zealand), as indicated by the rate of increase in consumer prices and by the recorded unemployment rates for the group.[1]

Whenever unemployment rose during the two preceding decades, governments took steps to reduce it by adopting expansionary measures; but in the later 1970s they generally allowed unemployment to remain high. This implies a belief on their part that any measures they took to reduce it would have caused intolerably high rates of inflation. In particular, they appear to have accepted the view that expansionary measures that had worked in earlier decades had somehow become incapable of reducing unemployment without seriously worsening inflation. But (as will be argued below) the problem appears to have been that the particular combinations of measures that governments had been using earlier in the 1970s, and continued to use to a considerable extent also in the late 1970s and early 1980s, exerted a greater upward pressure on prices, at any given level of unemployment, than the sort of combinations of measures that prevailed in the 1960s.

At any rate, the policies being pursued in the later 1970s and early 1980s clearly failed to solve the problem of stagflation.[2] Reasons will be given in Chapter 3 for the view that the prevailing combination of high and steadily rising tax rates (and high government outlays), with low or negative real post-tax interest rates, tends to exert upward pressure on the price level, at any given level of employment. There were other influences – such as the oil price rises and the slower rise in productivity in the 1970s – which made the problem harder to solve; and it could not reasonably be contended that the rise in inflation and unemployment that occurred in the 1970s was necessarily caused entirely by these changes in the setting of macroeconomic instruments since the 1960s. But real interest rates fell sharply in the later 1960s, and tax ratios were clearly rising then (well before the oil boom of the 1970s, or the slowing of productivity growth), and, as inflation began to speed up also at that time, the evidence supports the view that the increases in tax rates and the reductions in real post-tax interest rates exerted an upward pressure on the price level (at any given level of employment). So far as this is true, an essential element in any policy to cure stagflation is thus to return the setting of taxation and real post-tax interest rates to somewhere close to that which prevailed during the 1960s.

Table 2.2 provides part of the evidence by showing the sharp rise in tax revenue as a percentage of total output (as measured by Gross Domestic Product – 'GDP').[3] For reasons that will be discussed in the next chapter, the cost-inflationary effects of these high tax rates tended to raise the price level at any given level of activity (by comparison with a mix with tighter money or lower government spending). In addition, many forms of government spending also presumably have an upward effect on prices, so that a rise in the ratio of those types of government outlay to total incomes is likely also to have an inflationary effect. The level of government spending (on various definitions) did not show as much upward trend in relation to GDP as was shown by taxation; and the increases in it were partly because private spending had been depressed as a result of the general setting of policy. But government spending was generally high (by past standards) in relation to total output (though that ratio varied greatly, according to the definitions used, in most countries over the 1970s). Where government outlays were of types that tended to raise the price level at any given level of employment, this factor would clearly reinforce the effects of the high tax rates.

The upward pressure on the price level (at each level of employment) exerted by rising tax rates (and probably also by most forms of high government spending) might have been offset by a sufficiently tight monetary policy, in the sense of high real interest rates. But nominal interest rates in the 1970s failed to keep pace with the rise in inflation, so that real returns to lenders and real costs to borrowers were low or even negative, especially after tax, for most of the 1970s. Table 2.3 shows an estimate for the real long-term bond rate (the relationship between long-term government bond rates and the rate of increase in consumer prices) in the principal OECD countries both before and after tax rates of 33⅓ per cent and 40 per cent (these rates being chosen as somewhere near the average of prevailing direct tax rates). After being clearly above the rate of inflation in the mid 1960s, long-term bond rates before tax were only just above the rate of inflation in

TABLE 2.1: INFLATION AND UNEMPLOYMENT IN THE OECD AREA

	1965	1966	1967	1968	1969	1970	1971	1972	1973	1974	1975	1976	1977	1978	1979	1980
Rise in Consumer prices (%)	3	3	3	4	5	6	5	5	8	13	11	9	9	8	10	13
Unemployment rate	3	3	3	3	3	3	4	4	3	3	5	5	5	5	5	6

Sources: OECD, *Economic Outlook*, various issues and *Towards Full Employment and Price Stability* (McCracken Report), OECD, 1977. The unemployment rates cover about 90% of the OECD total, and are adjusted to international definitions by the OECD.

TABLE 2.2: TAX REVENUE AS A RATIO OF GDP IN OECD COUNTRIES (%)

1965	1966	1967	1968	1969	1970	1971	1972	1973	1974	1975	1976	1977	1978	1979
27	28	29	29	30	31	31	31	32	33	34	35	36	36	37

Source: OECD, *Government Revenue in OECD Countries*, 1980.

TABLE 2.3: ESTIMATED LONG-TERM BOND RATE IN SEVEN MAJOR OECD COUNTRIES

	1965	1966	1967	1968	1969	1970	1971	1972	1973	1974	1975	1976	1977	1978	1979	1980
Real bond rate:																
pre-tax	3	3	3	2	3	2	2	2	0	−4	−2	1	0	2	0	−1
post-tax with a 40% tax rate	0	0	1	0	0	−1	−1	0	−3	−7	−5	−3	−3	−2	−4	−5
with a 33⅓% tax rate	1	1	1	0	0	0	0	0	−3	−7	−4	−2	−2	−1	−3	−4

Source: Derived from (partly unpublished) OECD data, and rounded to nearest whole number.

the early 1970s, and fell well below it in 1973–5. In 1976–8 long-term bond rates before tax were sometimes below and sometimes just above the rate of inflation. In 1979–80 nominal rates began to exceed the rate of inflation again, but were generally not sufficiently above it to yield a positive real return to the lender after tax. Throughout the 1970s, real post-tax interest rates were generally negative for most taxpayers; and even pre-tax real interest rates were sometimes negative, and throughout the decade were well below those that generally prevailed in the 1960s.

The evidence indicates that during the later 1970s governments kept tax rates high – or even increased them – and did not generally permit nominal interest rates to rise to the point where most lenders could obtain a reasonable positive real post-tax return on their financial assets (compared with about 1% in the mid-1960s). The consequent inflation led them to try to correct the excessive expansion of the quantity of money (in the mid-1970s especially), by which governments had kept nominal interest rates below the rate of inflation.

But high tax rates were the main means used in the later 1970s to check the growth in the quantity of money (rather than a tight monetary policy operating through the offer of bonds at attractive real rates of return). This method of holding down the rate of increase in the quantity of money had a relatively slight downward effect on inflation, and thus a relatively greater effect in the direction of increasing unemployment. In other words, the combination of measures chosen made it necessary to permit a very high rate of unemployment if it was hoped to reduce the rate of inflation by that means.

THE RISK OF CURRENT POLICIES BECOMING SELF-PERPETUATING

The policies pursued in most OECD countries in the late 1970s and early 1980s thus involved trying to hold down inflation by tolerating 'temporarily' high levels of unemployment, and doing it by means of a combination of macroeconomic measures – high tax rates and government spending, and low or negative real post-tax interest rates – that was very different from that which prevailed in the 1960s. It is doubtful whether unemployment as high as that prevailing at the beginning of the 1980s was in fact having any appreciable effect in restraining inflation (by comparison with a slightly lower level of unemployment); and it was at least possible that what effect the unemployment may have had in restraining wage increases was offset in its effects on the price level by the high unit costs that were the result of so many industries operating at well below capacity, and by the upward effects on prices of the protectionism that was being fostered in so many countries by the widespread recession.

Moreover, the choice of mix (a high budget and low real post-tax interest rates) was also exerting upward pressure on prices, which has also weakened any restraining effect on inflation that may have been the result of the high unemployment.

Yet the continued high rates of inflation made governments reluctant to adopt expansionary measures, and resigned to tolerating high unemployment. There was thus a risk that, unless there was a sharp break from the prevailing policies, the problem could be self-perpetuating: a vicious circle in which stagflation itself led to the continuation of deflationary policies, operated by means of misguided mixes of macroeconomic measures, and intensified by protectionism – leading to still more stagflation. This risk was the greater so far as governments reacted to rising budget deficits (as revenue fell and social services outlays increased as a result of the recession) by introducing still more contractionary budgets, often with still higher cost-increasing taxes.

OBJECTIVES AND PSEUDO-OBJECTIVES

The macroeconomic problems of the 1970s and early 1980s were to a considerable extent due to the emphasis placed by governments on subsidiary 'targets', rather than on the real aims of macroeconomic policy.

The goals of macroeconomic policy are primarily to check inflation and to minimise unemployment. (The state of the balance of payments is not important in itself, but only for the ways in which it may affect a country's ability to achieve the basic aims of macroeconomic policy in the long run.) But, unfortunately, governments have often set themselves other 'macroeconomic' aims – such as achieving a certain rate of growth of the quantity of money (on some definition), or a certain exchange rate, or a certain (maximum) level of rates of interest, or a certain (maximum) figure for the 'budget deficit' (in Britain, usually the 'Public Sector Borrowing Requirement'). They may do this in the expectation that the achievement of these goals of policy will in some way contribute towards achieving the fundamental macroeconomic goals of minimising inflation and unemployment; but such subsidiary objectives often attain a political importance in their own right, which makes it correspondingly more difficult for a government to concentrate on the real macroeconomic objectives. For if a government uses its limited number of macroeconomic-policy instruments to achieve those targets it cannot (except by the merest chance) be directing them also towards achieving the real macroeconomic goals of high employment and low inflation. Indeed, because governments have insufficient instruments to enable them also to achieve also these spurious, self-imposed, targets, a course of action that is likely to minimise unemployment and inflation may at times be considered politically 'impossible', simply because it would involve departing from one or more of the pseudo-macroeconomic objectives the government has set itself. Very often particular courses of action are opposed or avoided simply because they seem likely to make it harder to achieve one of these pseudo-macroeconomic objectives. For example, it may be said that a certain policy will make the budget deficit rise above the figure that 'the market' – or 'financial opinion' – happens at present to consider to be the maximum tolerable. But a government that makes this sort of aim its criterion of action cannot reasonably expect also to have a successful macroeconomic policy in terms of achieving the real macro objectives of minimising both inflation and unemployment.

The discussion of the present book is therefore devoted to considering the principles on which governments should act if their aim is to achieve the real macroeconomic objectives. If in a particular country this involves prejudicing the achievement of a particular subsidiary (pseudo-macroeconomic) target – for the rise in the quantity of money, or for interest rates, or the budget deficit, for example – it is important that this conflict should be brought out into the open, so that it can be widely and clearly understood that it is the adherence to the pseudo-macroeconomic objectives that is standing in the way of implementing a rational macroeconomic policy for achieving the fundamental objectives of high employment and low inflation.

Full employment and price stability as a dual aim

The commonly accepted way of thinking about these two objectives of macroeconomic policy that has evolved in recent decades is one in which inflation and unemployment have come to be widely thought of as conflicting aims, at least in the short run. So far as inflation is more likely to occur when unemployment falls very low, this assumption is defensible in periods of high employment, but much less defensible in recessions. Moreover, as the amount of inflation experienced during any period is influenced also by factors quite apart from the level of unemployment, this approach may be very dangerous; for it leads people to believe that the *only* way to stop inflation is to tolerate unemployment. Indeed, that assumption seems to have been the basis of the approach of most government in the OECD world in the later 1970s and early 1980s; though they often assert that in the long run there is no conflict; that the unemployment that they are permitting or creating will, by keeping down inflation, make it possible to restore a lower level of unemployment in the future (though they do not usually explain how this will happen). Yet there is no clear line of cause and effect through which higher unemployment in the present and the near future can be confidently expected to lead to less unemployment in the long run; and there is a risk that such policies may lead to permanently higher unemployment. Moreover, as will be argued below, there are other and better ways of reducing the upward pressure on the price level than by creating or tolerating more unemployment than would otherwise have been felt necessary, even if it could be assumed (which it cannot) that the higher unemployment will necessarily be effective in checking inflation, and that inflation will not increase when unemployment is subsequently reduced.

When a government concentrates its policies mainly on achieving only one aim of macro policy – reducing inflation, for example – whether or not it succeeds, it will almost certainly have an adverse effect on the other main macro objective (in this case, that of full employment): just as an equally single-minded (or disproportionate) direction of all its policy instruments towards reducing unemployment is almost certain to make inflation worse.

It is therefore essential that governments, and all those who discuss macroeconomic policy issues, should focus their attention firmly and consistently on the *dual* aim of minimising both inflation and unemployment, choosing the combination of measures that is likely to do most to achieve this dual aim. This involves constantly asking whether a particular setting of two or more instruments is likely to do more than the alternatives available to minimise the upward pressure on prices during the period in question ('the rate of inflation', as generally understood) for any given level of unemployment; or to minimise the amount of unemployment associated with any given amount of inflation.

In general, *any* change in the setting of a single instrument of policy will almost certainly be 'right' in one sense and 'wrong' in another so long as there is both excessive inflation and excessive unemployment. It will therefore always be possible to criticise any particular policy change (whether actual or contemplated) on the grounds that it will make it harder to achieve one basic aim or the other. But it will (for similar reasons) also be possible to defend the taking of *any* particular policy action on the grounds that it will promote the achievement of *either* less unemployment *or* less inflation. Most policy actions and their likely effects are usually discussed individually, so that this sort of circular and fruitless discussion constitutes the bulk of what is said or written about macroeconomic policy. The first step towards a more rational debate on current macroeconomic issues is, therefore, always to discuss a proposed change of the setting of one policy instrument (a tax cut, for example) in the context of the corresponding changes in other instruments that it will – and should – make possible, or which it will necessitate (perhaps a tighter monetary policy than would otherwise have been chosen); and then to ask whether the *combined* change in *both* policy instruments will be likely to lead to a closer approximation to the achievement of the desired *dual* objective of minimising both unemployment and inflation than will any alternative combination of measures.

Will unemployment check inflation?

In marked contrast to the approach to macroeconomic policy that has just been suggested, most governments have based their policies for tackling inflation on having a higher level of unemployment than they would otherwise have been willing to tolerate. But it is by no means generally true that the assumption underlying such policies is valid.

The view that a relatively high level of unemployment tends to check inflation depends largely upon its expected effect in restraining the rise in money wage rates. This, in turn, depends on the weight given by union negotiators to the interests of those people who may be taken out of the ranks of the employed if wage increases are excessive; for wage increases will normally continue to benefit those trade unionists who remain employed, even if unemployment rises at the same time. But it seems likely that fear of the loss of jobs tends to moderate wage claims and wage settlements – to some greater or smaller degree.

But, even assuming that unemployment usually slows down wage increases, that does not necessarily check inflation. One reason is that the people who are no longer producing goods and services will still be consuming – though presumably at lower levels than when they were employed. The more generous the unemployment benefits or the other social security incomes they receive, and the greater the extent to which they can borrow from others, or the extent of the resources of their own on which they can draw, the greater is the risk that there will be a rise in demand relative to supply, or, at any rate, no *downward* effect on the price level.

Furthermore, once unemployment rises to a reasonably high level, there may well be a substantial rise in average costs of production, as the fixed costs of firms have to be spread over a smaller output. So far as prices are influenced by the firm's unit costs, this may also be a factor tending to hold up the price level.

Even if it is 'normal' costs – average costs over the whole cycle – that firms consider when setting prices, this argument holds good; for the toleration of higher unemployment with a view to checking inflation will lead to a higher average level of unemployment – or at least to a larger proportion of 'recession' years in the cycle.

It would be reasonable to suppose that when unemployment is very *low*, a small rise in unemployment tends to reduce the upward pressure on prices. But if there are many people already unemployed, and if a large number of businesses are operating below capacity, a small rise in unemployment is less likely to restrain inflation than when the economy is operating nearer to full employment.

Moreover, there are many overhead costs involved in running the public sector of the economy – the defence services, most of the apparatus of government, including overseas expenditure on diplomatic representation, the postal and telephone services, for example – which have to be spread over a lower level of output in the private sector when there is widespread under-utilisation of capacity and of the work force. This means that all these various services have to be financed by levying correspondingly higher tax rates during a recession on the reduced numbers at work, and higher tax rates on each unit of goods and services produced. The correspondingly higher tax rates, and for postal and telephone services the higher unit charges, thus raise unit costs and so prices throughout the economy. This means that when the economy is in recession there is considerable scope to increase output whilst reducing unit costs and unit charges made for the financing of the public sector, as well as the scope there may be for reducing unit costs in private firms.

But even if it could be assumed that a high level of unemployment tends to check inflation, there would not be a case for tolerating the high unemployment if there are other ways of reducing inflation. (The next chapter will argue that there are, in fact other ways of reducing inflation without permitting temporarily high unemployment.) Some people appear to believe that a relatively high level of unemployment will be effective in restraining inflation, and that it is the only way of doing so; for them it therefore constitutes the necessary price for dealing with inflation. That view is essentially irreconcilable with the alternative view that there are other ways of handling the problem. For if there are other ways, it is illogical – and indefensible – to tolerate any unemployment above the minimum necessary for the efficient functioning of the economy.

In a situation of stagflation, policy should always be directed towards the dual aim of minimising inflation at any given level of unemployment; or (if unemployment does help to reduce inflation) towards minimising the amount of unemployment that is needed to bring down inflation by any given amount over a particular period. Those who feel that a relatively high level of unemployment is necessary (for a limited period) in order to reduce inflation, and also those who do not, presumably ought to be able to agree that if there are combinations of measures that will minimise the extent of inflation at any given level of unemployment it must be preferable to adopt them. Yet failure to pay attention to these considerations has repeatedly led governments to an excessively inflationary use of monetary weapons, in the misguided hope that this will hold down interest rates.

MONETARY POLICY AND INTEREST RATES

Throughout the post-war period governments have almost invariably been reluctant and tardy about letting nominal interest rates rise when inflation became worse, and have therefore kept monetary policy easy enough to hold nominal interest rates down – at least temporarily. But *real* interest rates cannot in practice be held down by this means for long; for the easy monetary policy tends to cause upward pressure on prices (at any given level of activity), and this causes nominal interest rates also to rise before long.[4] The reason why this argument has not become generally accepted among economists is presumably that the channel through which easy monetary policies exert this upward pressure on prices has not been adequately spelt out in the literature. Two of the main channels through which it has presumably been operating, especially during the 1970s will be discussed in Chapter 3 (see pp. 30–9). For our present purposes, it is sufficient to note that easy monetary policies tend to exert upward pressure on the price level at any given level of activity, and that, though they may hold down interest rates in the short run, they eventually make nominal interest rates higher by raising the actual and expected rate of inflation over the ensuing period, and probably have little or no effect on real interest rates in the longer run. But each delay in permitting nominal rates to rise with inflation makes the inflation itself worse; so that real interest rates have often been kept low, or even negative, for long periods during the 1970s and early 1980s; and this helps to explain why inflation continued at high rates, despite the high levels of unemployment.

As Dennis Robertson once put it:

> if governments do not see fit to pay rather higher interest rates because capital is scarce they may easily find themselves having to pay much higher rates in a desperate attempt to keep pace with the foreseen depreciation of money.[5]

16 *Unemployment, Inflation and New Macroeconomic Policy*

Definition of 'monetary policy'

A dangerously misleading definition of 'monetary policy' has gained widespread currency in recent years. This is the definition that equates the term with 'the change in the quantity of money'. The alternative – and older – definition that is employed in this book defines the term as meaning *the instruments of central banking control*, including bond operations and all those central banking instruments that operate through making the banks more or less able and willing to lend.

There are two main reasons for using the term 'monetary policy' only in the second sense. One is that a given rise in the quantity of money brought about as a result of budgetary operations – cuts in tax revenue, or rises in government outlays – may have very different effects from those of the same increase in the quantity of money brought about by monetary policy (bond purchases by the central bank). In order to discuss the mix of measures adequately, therefore, it is necessary to contrast monetary policy in this sense with each of the two budgetary measures. Moreover, a change on the budgetary side may or may not be complemented by an increase or reduction in the quantity of money: for a given reduction of tax revenue, therefore, a central bank will be able to decide how far the quantity of money shall be allowed to increase, and how far more bonds should be offered to the public – which is a decision of monetary policy. The second main reason for using the term 'monetary policy' in this sense (rather than to mean merely a change in the quantity of money) is that factors outside the government's control also affect the quantity of money; so that a faster rate of increase in it does not necessarily indicate any easing of monetary policy, and should certainly not be interpreted as necessarily *indicating* an easing of monetary policy – though that usage is often found in public discussion.

In the ensuing chapters, therefore, the term 'tighter monetary policy' will be used to mean a decision to sell rather more bonds to the public (or to buy fewer bonds from them) *for any given setting of the budget*, and 'an easing of monetary policy' will mean a decision to create rather more money and sell rather fewer bonds (again, with a given setting of budgetary policy).

It is strange that monetarist economists should have been responsible for the recent widespread practice of interpreting an actual rise in the quantity of money as indicating an easing of monetary policy. For they have been foremost in emphasising that an actual rise in *interest rates* should not be interpreted as necessarily meaning that monetary policy has been tightened. Yet it is equally true that both these indicators can change for reasons quite unrelated to decisions of monetary policy.

It is therefore essential that policy makers should not interpret an increase

Current Macroeconomic Problems and Policies 17

(or a faster rate of growth) in the quantity of money as being necessarily an indication that monetary policy has been eased – any more than a fall in interest rates should be interpreted as meaning that there has been an easing of monetary policy. Each of these 'indicators' is thoroughly misleading as a guide to whether there has been any change in the setting of monetary policy; and it is still less defensible to *define* an easing of monetary policy to mean a faster rise in the quantity of money (or a reduction in interest rates). For much the same reasons, the budget deficit can also be affected by many things other than budgetary policy, and is therefore no sort of guide to the direction or extent of any changes in budgetary policy (a matter that will be discussed in more detail in Chapter 5). All these 'indicators' should thus be avoided like the plague, for they give no reliable indication of either the present setting of policy or of the way in which it ought to be changed. Until people cease to misuse them, however, it will be very difficult to secure the adoption, and public acceptance, of more rational macroeconomic policies. One reason for this is that the combination of measures chosen to achieve a given reduction in the rate of increase of the quantity of money may itself have a considerable bearing on whether the monetary targets will be met; so that failure to consider the best way of aiming at that target often makes it harder to operate such a policy successfully. Even if governments continue to set themselves monetary targets, it is thus essential for them to pay at least as much attention to the combination of measures with which they seek to meet those targets.

CONTROLLING THE MONETARY AGGREGATES

The emphasis placed in many countries during the later 1970s upon target rates of increase for the quantity of money (on some definition or other) implies that the central bank and the government can reasonably be expected to control these monetary aggregates. But the experience of a number of countries in recent years has shown that this is far from easy.

There may be political obstacles standing in the way of governments exercising enough restraint in their own spending, or of their pursuing a tight enough monetary policy, to achieve the intended results. But, quite apart from these political obstacles, there may also be technical difficulties. In particular, the quantity of money may well be in large measure determined by the demand for money in the private sector. This means that when businesses find themselves short of funds they may find ways of borrowing more from banks, and banks may find it hard or impossible to hold down the rise in bank deposits. In countries such as Britain and Australia, where the overdraft method of bank lending is used extensively, this may take the form of borrowers making fuller use than usual of their right to borrow from banks by overdrawing their accounts – and a consequent rise in the quantity of money. Under the system of loans, which is more common in the USA and elsewhere, it is presumably easier for the central bank to keep control of the volume of bank deposits – and so the recorded quantity of money. But the underlying monetary realities, as distinct from the statistical magnitudes, are really no different as between the two systems; it is merely that the measured monetary aggregates have a different significance in a country where overdrafts are the most common form of bank lending from that which they have in one where loans are the main method used for extending bank credit.

If the level of bank lending and the rate of increase in the quantity of money is partly determined by demand factors, it is obviously correspondingly harder for a government to make monetary targets a firm basis for its macroeconomic policy. It seems wisest to acknowledge that both demand and supply factors are of importance; and the relative extent of each is a matter about which there is much room for argument. But, at the very least, as a contribution to clear thought on the matter, we should stop referring to the actual quantity of money as 'the money supply' – which begs this vital issue of how far the *actual* quantity of money can be controlled (whether from the demand or supply side).[6]

The relevance of these matters to the main subject-matter of this book is that the particular combination of macroeconomic instruments employed may itself have a bearing on the ability of a government to control the rate of increase in the monetary aggregates, and also on the significance of any particular monetary aggregates.

In particular, it is probable that one reason why central banks often found it hard to control the growth of the principal monetary aggregates during the later 1970s was that the mix of measures was such as to give potential borrowers a strong incentive to borrow from their banks as much as they could. For the generally high level of tax rates imposed a severe strain on company liquidity, whilst it also meant that, so far as they were paying tax on profits, the interest that they were paying their banks was worth a good deal as a tax deduction. Post-tax interest rates to these borrowers were thus relatively low in real terms, even with overdraft rates in double figures, when inflation was also at or near double-digit levels, provided that the borrowing was to finance untaxed capital gains or some other untaxed benefit, such as ending or avoiding a strike.

By contrast, high tax rates and high and unpredictable rates of inflation make it less attractive to borrow at long-term, and also difficult to raise long-term funds. High tax rates erect a 'wedge' between lenders and the earnings of borrowers – with the lenders being taxed on their interest receipts, even when these are, at least partly, merely a compensation for the real loss inflicted on the lenders as a result of holding a financial asset fixed in money terms during a period of inflation. In such circumstances, the long-term capital market allocates resources very inefficiently, and it is not surprising that businesses feel impelled to borrow as much of their requirements as possible (on shorter term) from their banks. By borrowing at shorter term they at least know that if inflation comes down, their nominal interest rate payments will come down with it; whereas if they borrow at long term, and inflation then comes down, they may be saddled for a long time with very high *real* rates of interest. In such circumstances, it is naturally difficult for governments to reduce the scale of bank borrowing by businesses. A move towards lower tax rates, accompanied by temporarily higher interest rates, would be more likely to succeed in holding down the expansion of bank credit.

The need to pay high nominal interest rates (even though they were often low or negative in real after-tax terms) has been given as a reason why firms in Britain felt obliged to borrow extensively from their banks in the later 1970s and early in the 1980s – and those who argue in this way imply that firms would have actually borrowed *less* had interest rates been *lower*. But, even if that were true, the relevant question should be whether a reduction in tax rates would be likely to have a *greater* effect in reducing their borrowing from banks than would a cut in interest rates (resulting from an easier monetary policy) *having the same effect on real activity*: for high tax rates also increase the need to borrow from banks.

Moreover, the higher the tax rates and the lower the overdraft rates, the greater is the incentive to borrow on overdraft rather than on longer term; so that a shift to a mix with lower tax rates and higher overdraft rates makes bank borrowing likely to fall. One may acknowledge that both high interest rates *and* high taxes may make firms *seek* to borrow more – at least temporarily – in a period when their cash flow is low and sales prospects are weak; but this is not an argument for reducing interest rates rather than tax rates – for that is likely to be the *opposite* policy to that which would be most likely to reduce their bank borrowing. It is the failure to permit interest rates (after allowing for tax) to rise in step with the expected rate of inflation over the period of the bank borrowing that makes it relatively attractive for firms to borrow as much as they can from their banks, and so makes it harder to control the monetary aggregates.

DO PRESENT POLICIES MEAN PERMANENTLY HIGH UNEMPLOYMENT?

Governments do not usually admit that their policies are intended to create, or at least tolerate, unemployment, with the aim of thereby reducing the rate of inflation. It is evident, however, that the policies adopted with a view to checking inflation in the later years of the 1970s amounted to (at least) tolerating unemployment. Defenders of the policies would presumably assert that this was the fault of those who tried to raise their money incomes faster than productivity was increasing; and that restraint on the level of overall demand (or on the rate of increase in the quantity of money) is an essential part of the cure, even if it leads to some temporary unemployment for a while.

Whether one describes this as 'using unemployment with the aim of checking inflation', or whether one takes the view that the unemployment is wholly unintended by the governments concerned, and not really their fault, no-one can reasonably disagree that ways should be sought to minimise the amount and duration of unemployment that occurs in the process of reducing inflation. It is to this question that the discussion of the present book is therefore directed.

But it has become clear in recent years that unemployment at higher rates than for some forty years past is being tolerated for far longer than the governments applying the policies originally intended. This raises the possibility that current policies will in practice – if not in intention – turn out to be based on a *permanently* higher level of unemployment, rather than on a merely *temporary* increase in it.

Indeed, one often hears suggestions that it will be impossible to return to the low levels of unemployment that prevailed in the 1950s and 1960s. If this view is coming to be accepted at all widely it therefore becomes relevant to compare the policy proposals in this book with the social and economic consequences of having *permanently* higher unemployment. Obviously, the costs of a policy relying on permanently high unemployment would be still greater than those of temporarily high unemployment. The benefit to be gained by making use of appropriate mixes of macroeconomic instruments at a high level of activity would thus be correspondingly greater if the alternative policy is that of tolerating high unemployment for an indefinite period (which now appears to be in fact the type of policy that is becoming established in most OECD countries). Even those who were prepared to tolerate a *temporary* rise in unemployment, in the hope that it would check inflation, should now presumably be much more prepared to consider the benefits of alternative policies, in view of the long period of high unemployment and under-capacity operation to which the recent policies have led in many countries.

A simple 'U-turn' is no solution

A reversal of the self-defeating and potentially self-perpetuating policies prevailing at the start of the 1980s would involve the recognition by the governments of the principal OECD countries (and by public opinion generally in those countries) that the sort of policies generally applied in the last half-decade or so have been doing little or nothing to improve the general macroeconomic situation in the world economy.

But, at the same time, it is equally important that when policy changes are made, those changes should not be along the lines of most of the widely publicised alternative policies – including those advocated by political oppositions, and many trade unions and business organisations – which involve relying unduly on easing monetary policy or on raising government spending; for those types of approach would certainly make inflation worse, whether or not they had any lasting effect in reducing unemployment.

Rather than *either* a continuation of the present policies *or* the sort of reversal of policy (sometimes called a 'U-turn' in Britain) that seems to be favoured by the most vocal critics of current policies, the approach that is required is one that constantly seeks the best combination of measures to minimise stagflation, using tight monetary measures to control inflation and general tax cuts to reduce both cost-inflation and unemployment. This would amount to a sharp reversal of the prevailing ways of thinking about macroeconomic policy in most countries, though it is consistent with many aspects of the policy introduced early in 1981 by the Reagan Administration in the USA. That approach, however, did not greatly cut real tax rates, its main effect being to prevent effective income tax rates from rising with inflation, as they would otherwise have done; it was thus – in this respect – no better than a small move in the right direction. But it did accompany the original announcement of the tax cuts with the expressed intention of keeping monetary policy tight; and its search for forms of government spending that could be cut as excessive was certainly consistent with the present proposals – but only if cuts in government expenditure are to be combined with tax cuts on a large enough scale to ensure that there is a reduction in unemployment. The Reagan policy announced in early 1981 was, then, not so much a possible cure for stagflation as merely an adjustment in the setting of macroeconomic instruments in such a way that they might cease to make stagflation worse.

CONCLUSION

The discussion in this chapter has pointed out that the macroeconomic policies pursued in the later 1970s and early 1980s apparently did little or nothing to solve the problem of high unemployment coupled with high rates of inflation. This was essentially because they were directed merely at influencing the overall level of demand – which had been the appropriate way of tackling the situations of *either* high unemployment *or* excess demand of earlier decades – but which was inappropriate for dealing with the dual problem of stagflation. Moreover, the combination of rising taxation, high government spending and low or negative real post-tax interest rates contrasted markedly with the setting of these instruments in earlier decades (when macroeconomic policy had been more successful). The next chapter will present arguments in support of the view that a setting of these instruments such as prevailed in the 1970s could reasonably have been expected to exert a greater upward pressure on the price level (at any given level of employment) than the settings of these instruments that was general in the 1960s.

The best hope for dealing with the persistent problem of stagflation is, therefore, for governments and all those who discuss macroeconomic policy to transform their approach to these issues into one that consistently seeks for the best combination of instruments for stopping stagflation: that is, for minimising the upward pressure on the price level at any given level of unemployment, and for holding down unemployment with the least possible upward pressure on prices.

3 The Basic Proposals

The proposals for resolving the present crisis in macroeconomic policy that are put forward in this book are based on the simple proposition that some policies for reducing unemployment are less inflationary (or more likely to reduce inflation) than are others. So long as this is true, a change in the direction of giving more stimulus in the *least* inflationary way, coupled with an offsetting movement of some other instrument (one that is likely to cause *more* inflation for a given stimulus) in a relatively contractionary direction, can reduce the upward pressure on prices at any given level of unemployment. It is therefore not necessary for either form of stimulus *taken alone* to exert downward pressure on the price level. Even if it is true that a particular (high) level of unemployment will help to check inflation (a view that may or may not be defensible, depending partly on the instruments used to raise unemployment), the speed with which that aim will be achieved at that level of unemployment depends partly on the combination of measures used.

The three broad groups of macroeconomic instruments available are: (1) monetary policy – central banking instruments that operate mainly by way of official purchases and sales of bonds, but also by making it relatively easier and cheaper (or harder and more costly) to borrow from banks; (2) taxation; and (3) government spending. The simpler division into monetary policy on the one hand and budgetary on the other is both inadequate and misleading for the purpose of dealing with stagflation. For the two groups of *budgetary* instruments are likely to have contrasting effects: a stimulus provided by way of a tax cut is likely to be the *least* inflationary form of stimulus, whereas one provided by means of a rise in government spending on goods and services will normally be one of the *most* inflationary. This important distinction is blurred if one speaks of budgetary policy as a single instrument incorporating *both* taxation and government spending, or if one judges the setting of policy by such inadequate and misleading indicators as the budget deficit (or Public Sector Borrowing Requirement in Britain).

Various hypotheses may be put forward about the relative effects on prices (for a given effect on employment) of changing each of the alternative instruments; and one can suggest ways in which some tax cuts will be more likely than others to curb inflation, or some forms of government spending more likely to increase it, for any given effect on employment. Provided that there is some foreseeable difference in the impact on prices during the period in question, for a given effect on employment, as between one instrument and another, however, it is indefensible to permit a temporarily higher level of unemployment than would otherwise have been chosen, merely with the aim of checking inflation; for there will then always be some switch of the mix that would have the same effect on prices without the loss of output and the social suffering that result from the temporarily high unemployment.

The particular form of these proposals advanced in this chapter is that, on the basis of only one or two very simple assumptions, the most appropriate way of stopping stagflation is to cut tax rates and keep monetary policy relatively tight, though allowing the net effect of the change of policy to be expansionary. A second form of mix that may be expected to work in the same way would be a simultaneous cut in the ratio of both government spending and taxation to total income or output (which need not necessarily mean an eventual reduction in the absolute level of either of them if the alternative is high unemployment). A third mix, which may work in some circumstances, is a very tight monetary policy coupled with a *rise* in the *ratio* of government spending to total output. The mixes that politicians – whether on the right or left of politics – have seemed to prefer in most countries in recent years are generally contrary to those being proposed here. They have preferred to ease monetary policy (even at the cost of keeping taxes high) wherever they felt it safe to do so; they have found it hard (even where they have been willing in principle) to reduce the ratio of government spending to total output; and they have been unwilling to cut appreciably the ratio of tax revenue to total income. They have certainly been generally unwilling to keep monetary policy very tight – which would be necessary if a high level of government spending were not to lead to high rates of inflation.

The proposals put forward in this chapter thus have nothing inherently of the 'right' or 'left' of politics about them. There are different forms of them that should appeal to parties of either the right or the left, at least in certain respects (such as the relatively greater or smaller emphasis of different mixes on the role of the public sector). But basically they are each in conflict in certain other respects with the views of most politicians, at least as exemplified by the policies of major parties of most OECD countries (except perhaps West Germany, Austria and Switzerland) during the 1970s. In particular, they are in sharp conflict with the current preference (especially on the 'right' of politics) for trying to stop inflation by creating or tolerating high unemployment; and they are also in sharp conflict with the views of those on the 'left' who hope to solve the problem largely by higher government spending and easy money, with relatively high tax rates.

GOOD AND BAD FORMS OF STIMULUS

The inflationary effects of certain forms of stimulus usually employed in the past – increased government spending financed by creating money rather than selling bonds, or easy monetary policies, in particular – have led many people to be sceptical about the feasibility of a government taking *any* sort of appropriate action to restore full employment without this leading to more inflation. But this is not a rational view; for to argue that 'governments cannot cure unemployment by throwing money at it' is not a rational objection to *non-inflationary* ways of reducing unemployment. The trouble is that in the past economists and journalists (and all who think and talk about macroeconomic policy) have failed to distinguish adequately between *inflationary* forms of expansion and *anti-inflationary* ones: and it is inflationary forms of stimulus that have almost invariably been employed. People have thus been able to point to deficiencies in the more inflationary forms of stimulus and to misuse them as an argument against *any* form of stimulus, simply because the relative effects on prices and employment of the various policy instruments has not been widely understood.

We turn now to considering the basic assumptions on which the above policy prescriptions are based: (i) the cost-increasing effects of high tax rates; (ii) the price-increasing effects of low real post-tax interest rates; and (iii) the price-increasing effects of many forms of government outlay.

The Basic Proposals for Stopping Stagflation

A. If taxes have cost-increasing effects (not shared by tight monetary policies or by reductions in government spending), cut taxes and keep monetary policy tight enough to check inflation, or cut taxes and also cut the ratio of government spending to total output.

B. If a tighter monetary policy has price-reducing effects that are not fully shared by budgetary measures having the same effect on employment, tighten monetary policy and make budgetary policy more expansionary (preferably by way of tax cuts).

At the same time, give a net stimulus by making the overall setting of budgetary and monetary instruments sufficiently expansionary. The greater the additional upward pressure on prices that is expected to result from a given fall in unemployment, the greater the necessary switch of mix that should accompany the stimulus.

THE VARIOUS COST-INFLATIONARY EFFECTS OF HIGH TAX RATES

There are various ways in which high tax rates may increase cost inflation. Any one of these effects would in itself be sufficient to justify the use of a mix involving tax cuts; but as each of them is potentially important it is inappropriate to base the case for or against the use of such a mix on any one of them alone. The writer knows of no evidence that would justify emphasising one of these groups of effects as being more important than the others. Efforts to estimate the relative cost-inflationary effect – measured over a sufficiently long run – of different types of taxes would be useful; but it is difficult to envisage ways of measuring the relative importance of the various channels through which high taxes increase costs and prices, for most taxes operate (to some greater or lesser extent) through all the channels.

1. The first such channel is through effects on productivity. These include the diversion of effort to administering, enforcing, avoiding and evading taxes, with consequent downward effects on the output of other goods and services (at each level of employment and incomes). They include all the distortions to the pattern of consumption and production that taxes inevitably cause. (Effects through incentives may be placed on one side – beloved though they are of politicians; for we do not know whether, on balance, they are positive or negative.)
2. *Even if there were no such productivity effects*, high taxes tend to raise costs and wage rates (by comparison with a tight monetary policy having the same effect on employment), quite apart from any effect they may have on the *relationships* between wages and profits.
3. *Even if there were no productivity effects, and no general upward effect on (both) costs and prices*, a high level of taxes, at least in forms that reduce post-tax real incomes, may force up pre-tax wage rates *relative to profits* (by comparison with a monetary policy having the same effect on employment). This would mean that higher levels of nominal demand (and consequently greater upward pressure on prices) would be needed to achieve any given level of employment.[1]

All these effects may be thought of as 'shifting the aggregate supply curve' – increasing the upward pressure on prices at each level of employment. (The term 'supply side effects' – often used of late, especially in the USA – is probably best reserved, in this context, for those cost-reducing effects of tax cuts that operate through productivity.)

It should be noted, however, that none of the effects described above depend upon the argument – which gained some currency in the USA in early 1981 – that tax concessions ought to be made mainly to the rich, so as to raise the propensity to save, in the hope that this would facilitate a higher level of investment. But any consequent rise in the propensity to save would reduce the incentive to invest, so far as it depended on consumption. Larger tax incentives for investment (and a larger budget deficit) would thus be needed to stimulate investment if the tax cuts were mainly for the rich. In any case, so long as there are such widespread unused resources the prime means of stimulating investment should be to bring the unused resources into production; and so long as resources are being used inefficiently (as a result of misguided resource allocation policies), a better use of resources makes possible higher investment without the necessity to reduce the consumption of either the poor or the rich.

The costs of evoision

When the high level of tax rates leads to avoidance and evasion, this imposes a number of costs on the community. These costs are incurred whether the problem is that of avoidance (changing one's activities in such a way as to reduce tax payable legally) or evasion (the illegal non-payment of taxes). Indeed, there is inevitably a 'grey' area between what is legal non-payment of taxes and what is illegal, for the line between them depends not only on changes in laws (and differences in laws between one country and another) but also on the decision of courts (past and current) and the administrative decision of officials. It is thus useful for present purposes to use the portmanteau word 'evoision' to cover both sorts of non-payment of taxes.

The most obvious cost is the time and effort devoted by people to finding ways of not paying their taxes: this could otherwise have been devoted either to producing more goods and services of types that the community is willing to purchase, or to leisure activities that would bring the individual more satisfaction.

A slightly less obvious cost is that one way of escaping the payment of taxes may be some form of barter: the electrician does a job for the plumber and vice versa. But the inefficiencies of barter are well known. Most of us are well aware that it is difficult (indeed, well-nigh impossible) to find someone who is willing to do a job that you want done who is himself or herself at the same moment requiring someone to do a job that you are willing and able to do for them at the real price implied by these two services. Moreover, when people have a preference for doing such work without being paid in money it becomes harder – and more costly – for others to persuade them to do a job in return for payment in money. The same result follows if people insist on

28 *Unemployment, Inflation and New Macroeconomic Policy*

payment in currency (rather than by cheque), as being harder for the taxman to trace, and this means that more scrupulous people find it costs more to buy the goods or services in question. This clearly reduces the efficiency with which the resources of the economy are employed, and raises the price of those transactions that are not settled for cash.

The widespread existence of evoision also involves the employment of large numbers of people in trying to enforce the existing tax laws, and in closing existing loopholes, or in trying to decide (whether in courts of law or in the course of administering the laws) what is legal and what is not. Again, this is a diversion of skilled manpower away from more useful work, and thus raises the costs of producing the types of goods and services that people would have preferred to purchase (but for the high level of taxes).

LAGS IN COST REDUCTIONS

Some people have commented on the proposal to reduce costs by tax cuts (accompanied by an appropriately tight monetary policy) that its effects will be only short-term, whereas others have argued that the favourable effects on productivity that might result would operate only in the long term. In fact, however, the various types of favourable effects on prices will be spread over widely differing time spans: and this constitutes an additional argument for making tax cuts general, rather than concentrating them on particular types of taxes.

The tax cuts likely to have the most immediate impact on indexes of inflation are ones in indirect taxes on items of mass consumption – general taxes on expenditure, such as value-added tax, sales-taxes, or taxes on conventional necessities such as beer and tobacco. Any forms of assistance to agriculture (such as the system of price-supports operated by the EEC) that operate by raising the price of foodstuffs to the consumer resemble an indirect tax, a reduction in which would have a marked effect in holding down indexes of retail prices, and so on household budgets. These effects may be expected to have an indirect impact in restraining money wage increases, mainly just after any consequent change has occurred in the indexes of consumer prices.

Cuts in taxes on the employment of labour (such as payroll taxes and employers' contributions to national insurance or social services), or taxes on business inputs such as petrol, may be expected to have some immediate impact so far as prices react to falls in costs, and some in the longer run – when businesses that are to some greater or lesser extent price-makers (rather than price-takers) revise their prices upwards. So far as reductions in

The Basic Proposals

the rate of increase in money wage rates occur only with a lag, there will likewise be a further lag before any such slowing down in wage increases works its way through to the prices of final products.

Cuts in income tax on persons may be expected to have some of their effect over the medium run, as wage demands and wage settlements are adjusted downwards in response to the rise in take-home pay (for any given pre-tax income). Similar effects on salaries, and on the incomes of the self-employed, may take somewhat longer to show themselves, and effects that operate through raising the post-tax incomes of corporate businesses, and so eventually of dividend earners, will take still longer, as dividends respond only with a lag to changes in companies' post-tax incomes.

Cuts in company ('corporation') tax may have some fairly immediate effect if pricing decisions of businesses respond to the scope that it gives them to pay any given yield to shareholders out of a smaller pre-tax income for the company (and, if personal income tax is cut simultaneously, to pay a given post-tax dividend out of a smaller pre-tax income to shareholders). To some extent businesses may think of taxes on their profits as a form of business cost; but, even if they do not, cuts in company/corporation tax will enable them to cover their costs out of a lower pre-tax revenue; and to that extent enable them to charge lower prices.

The various productivity effects that are to be expected from tax cuts may be spread over various periods, extending into the indefinite future. The general improvement in the allocation of resources should have some fairly immediate effects, but will extend into the longer period as it affects investment decisions. The improvement in the operation of the capital market (including that which results from the reduction in the incentive for people to try to move away from financial assets into real assets) will have some immediate effect in curbing inflation, but much of its effect will be long term, as the pattern of investment improves. Effects through reductions in tax avoidance and tax evasion may to some extent occur quickly – for there are always some people who will be persuaded of the virtues of honesty, or that the game is not worth the candle, when the reward for evoision is reduced; but with others the habits may be too deeply ingrained to be changed quickly. To some extent this effect will be very long run, as new individuals come into the work force, or into those income groups where the incentive for evoision is strong. For as the composition of these groups changes towards people who have never acquired these habits, there will eventually be favourable productivity effects as a result of the consequent reversion of effort (that of those who would have otherwise been tax evoiders and that of the law enforcers) to more useful purposes.

In all, then, it does not seem reasonable to argue (as is sometimes done) that effects of tax cuts in reducing costs will be *either* 'mainly short run' *or* 'mainly very long run'. Provided that the tax cuts are spread over a wide range of taxes, their effects will be felt over a very wide range of different time spans: and usually a critic who voices one of these objections is doing so as a result of having appreciated only one, or only a few, of the ways in which tax cuts may help to check inflation. It is important to stress that there is no prima facie reason to consider any one of these channels as being much more important than the others: weight should therefore be given to them all.

MONETARY POLICY, REAL ASSETS, AND THE PRICE LEVEL

A relatively easy monetary policy is likely to have certain upward effects on the price level (and so on the rate of inflation over the period in which it is being eased) compared with the establishment of the same level of employment by means of a relatively tighter monetary policy and a correspondingly easier budgetary policy (leaving aside for the moment the probable differences in the direct effects on prices of taxes and government spending respectively, which are considered in other sections of this chapter). This effect does not seem to have been considered to any great extent in the literature, except in the sense that monetarists emphasise the effects of a relatively rapid rise in the quantity of money (or what they often call 'the money supply') upon the price level; and a mix with a relatively expansionary monetary policy will bring about a relatively rapid rise in the quantity of money.

The association in people's minds between a rapid rise in the quantity of money and a rapid rise in prices, whether this link is rational or not in itself, could be sufficient to account for the connection between rapidly rising prices and a rapidly rising quantity of money; for if it is sufficiently widely held, such a belief becomes self-fulfilling. But such a belief would be unlikely to last long unless there were a firm underlying basis for it. It is thus important to ask what is the underlying basis for such a view? What exactly is the substratum of Cheshire cat underlying the grin?

Most people have become aware over the past decade of high rates of inflation that most financial assets are scarcely worth holding; for the real return on them after tax is usually very low or negative, whereas many durable real assets, such as real estate, gold and other precious metals, some types of furniture (especially antiques) and some consumer durables, are likely to hold their value, or to more than hold it, in real terms during a period of rapid inflation. Inflation in itself makes people readier to hold real assets because they constitute a better 'hedge' against inflation than do the available financial assets. If the yield on available financial assets went up fully in proportion to inflation there would not be any reason to expect such a switch towards those real assets and consequent upward pressure on their prices. But governments have often not been willing to allow interest rates to rise fully and speedily to levels that reflect the actual or expected rate of inflation; and because they have taxed that part of the interest paid on bonds which is not really income but merely compensation for the fall in real value of such assets resulting from inflation, people have become reluctant to hold as much by way of financial assets as they would have done if the real (post-tax) yield on them had been as high as in the past. In some countries governments have actually encouraged people to move towards holding more real estate by making interest paid on mortgages at least partly tax-deductible. Capital gains on owner-occupied houses are often also treated more favourably from a taxation point of view than are other forms of capital gains, especially those on financial assets, in those countries where capital gains are taxed.

But the vital question for macroeconomic policy is whether the upward pressure on the prices of these real assets that results from a relatively easy monetary policy (especially if accompanied by high tax rates on returns from financial assets) exerts upward pressure on the prices of goods and services *generally* (and not merely of those real assets that are widely held as preferable alternatives to bonds in times of inflation).

When we speak of 'the price level' or 'the rate of inflation' we are normally thinking of an index of prices that measures not the prices of existing real assets but only those of newly produced goods and services. But a rise in the prices of existing houses or existing bars of gold (for example) will raise also the prices of newly produced houses and newly produced gold.[2] It is true that if this reflected merely a switch in the level of real demand towards some items (houses and gold) and a comparable fall in demand for other items there would be offsetting falls in prices elsewhere – so far as this depended on demand factors. But the essential point is that *the sort of goods towards which people move as a hedge against inflation* (or as an alternative to holding financial assets) *are goods in relatively inelastic supply*; that is to say, it is because the output of such real assets as gold, or the supply of real estate, cannot be readily increased to meet any rise in demand for them that they are attractive to hold as real assets. As some newly produced goods are close substitutes for those that have consequently become attractive assets to hold, the price rise affects them also: and because these types of newly produced goods are items of which the supply cannot readily be increased on a sufficient scale to meet the rise in demand, the switch of demand towards these types of goods exerts upward pressure on real costs, and so on the price level generally.

If a government changes its policy to a mix that gives lenders a higher real return on financial assets, and maintains the general real of activity by reducing taxes generally, one result is therefore likely to be downward pressure on the prices of those types of goods (including most obviously real estate, gold, antiques and so on) that people hold instead of financial assets (in periods when the latter do not provide an attractive enough real yield to shield them against inflation). This downward pressure on prices may be expected to spread to the prices of those newly produced goods that are close substitutes for the types of goods held as alternatives to financial assets. This means that a reduction in the demand for such goods, and a rise in that for other goods and services, should lead to increased output of the latter, and downward pressure on the general price level (as a result of demand being switched towards those types of goods and services of which supplies can be increased more readily).

This switch of mix towards a tighter monetary policy but lower taxes (at any given level of total output or employment) may thus be expected to exert downward pressure on the prices of goods and services in general relative to those of financial assets – which will now have become more attractive. As governments usually try to hold down real interest rates by means of monetary measures, a decision to stop trying to hold down interest rates will normally be carried out by permitting a slower rise in the amount of money created by monetary policy; and a slower rise in the general price level may be expected to result.

Interest rates as a cost

The foregoing argument is not intended to deny that interest payments are a cost; higher interest rates add to the costs of business, as do also taxes on businesses. To that extent, both instruments have cost-increasing effects to set against their effects in restraining inflation by depressing demand. But the above argument is merely that if a tightening of monetary policy is compared with a rise in tax rates having the same effect in restraining business expenditure, and each having a broadly similar effect on business costs, the tightening of monetary policy will have certain downward effects on the price level (through the asset market) which tax increases do not have.

Real interest rates, nominal interest rates, taxation and inflation

If interest payments are not taxed, the real rate of interest received by the owner of a financial asset consists of the nominal rate of interest adjusted

The Basic Proposals 33

downwards appropriately for the rate of inflation. (Arithmetical examples are given in the box.)

> Suppose inflation were at 10 per cent per annum, a nominal rate of interest of 10 per cent would be required to maintain the real value of the asset intact in the face of inflation – without yielding any positive real return. If a return of 1 per cent in real terms were to be earned on the asset, a nominal rate of an additional 1.1 per cent (making 11.1 per cent in all) would be required (the additional 0.1 per cent to offset the fall in the real value of the money paid out in interest over the year in question).
>
> If the interest is taxed, naturally the pre-tax rate of interest must rise even faster than this in order to compensate the holder of the asset for the fall in its real value over a year in which there has been inflation. If the interest were taxed at a rate of 50 per cent, a pre-tax nominal return of 20 per cent would clearly be required in order to maintain the capital value of the asset intact (with a 10 per cent rate of inflation) (without any real return being earned on it). If a 1 per cent real yield were also to be earned, another 2.2 per cent of the original face value of the asset at the beginning of the year would be required in order to yield a real post-tax return of 1 per cent (making a total pre-tax interest of 22.2 per cent). If there were no inflation, a pre-tax interest of 2 per cent would have sufficed for the same purpose; so that (with a 50 per cent tax rate) a rise in inflation from 0 to 10 per cent necessitates a rise in the pre-tax rate of interest from 2 per cent to 22.2 per cent. Or, at the rate of 5 per cent inflation (nearer to that prevailing in the developed world during the 1960s), a pre-tax return of 10 per cent would have been needed to maintain the real value of the asset, and a return of 12.1 (10 + 2.1) in order to provide a yield of 1 per cent in real terms. With inflation doubling from 5 per cent to 10 per cent, therefore, the pre-tax rate of interest requires to increase – from 12.1 per cent to 22.2 per cent.
>
> In order to assess the effect of rising tax rates on interest – and so of rising proportions of interest-earners entering income groups where higher rates of tax are payable – take the case of a 10 per cent rate of inflation, and compare the effect of a 50 per cent income-tax rate (just considered) with one of 60 per cent. As we have seen, a 20 per cent pre-tax rate of return would have been needed in order to maintain capital intact in real terms when income tax was 50 per cent. To achieve the same effect with a tax rate of 60 per cent, the pre-tax yield has to rise to 25 per cent: in other words, a rise of only a fifth in the tax rate requires a rise of as much as a quarter in the pre-tax yield in order to maintain capital intact. If a given post-tax yield is to be earned on the asset, the pre-tax yield also has to rise faster than the tax rate. For we have seen that if a post-tax yield of 1 per cent was to be earned when inflation was at 10 per cent and when tax rates were only 50 per cent, an extra 2.2 per cent in pre-tax interest would be required (in addition to what was needed to keep capital intact); but with a tax rate as high as 60 per cent, the pre-tax yield has to rise more than in proportion (to 2.75 per cent).

The higher the tax rate (at any rate of inflation), the more must pre-tax nominal interest rates rise *relative to the rate of inflation* in order to maintain the real value of the asset in question, or to provide any given real post-tax return on the asset (as indicated by the examples in the box).

Yet very often pre-tax rates of interest have not even kept up with the rise in the rate of inflation. To some extent this is because (at least in the short run) not all lenders adjust their asset holdings to allow for the higher rate of inflation (perhaps partly because they may not expect that it will last), and borrowers do not want to commit themselves to paying higher nominal rates in case the rate of inflation comes down during the period of the loan. But probably more important is the reluctance of governments to allow those rates of interest that they influence or control to keep up with the most reasonable estimate of the prevailing rate of inflation. This is usually because the political pressure that can be exerted by borrowers (especially mortgage borrowers and businessmen) exceeds that which is normally exerted by lenders, especially the small savers who hold the securities and bank deposits that are most adversely affected in real value as a result of inflation.

The consequences of this are (1) that potential lenders have sought other ways of holding their assets, rather than in assets bearing a fixed rate of interest that did not keep up with inflation, and on which the nominal interest was being taxed (even though most or all of the interest was in fact merely a compensation for the fall in the real value of the asset); and (2) that governments have had to use other instruments, notably high tax rates, to try to restrain demand in the face of the low or negative real rates of interest.

Despite these considerations, when reference is made to real interest rates in the press, one usually sees reference only to *pre-tax* rates of interest – an 11 per cent rate of interest being referred to as 'positive' in real terms when inflation is 10 per cent, even though no rational investor liable to tax would think of such a yield as being positive, and many people who have probably never sat down to do the arithmetic are well aware that it is unwise to hold financial assets on which the yield is not properly adjusted for inflation in periods of high inflation and high taxation such as the 1970s. Every failure by governments to put pre-tax interest rates up – or to bring tax rates on the interest receipts down – in step with inflation increases the pressure on people to hold their accumulated assets in real forms (real estate, gold bars, antiques and so on), rather than financial ones; and this places upward pressure on the price level generally.

Are positive real post-tax interest rates enough?

When it is pointed out that during the 1970s real post-tax interest rates have often been negative – to an extent and for a length of time greatly in excess of any period since the war years and the early 1950s – the comment is sometimes made that for some owners of financial assets who are not subject to tax on their interest income, the real returns will have been positive; or that even post-tax rates may at some particular time have become positive (at least on some estimates).

It is therefore important to emphasise that the negative real rates that existed in many countries for at least part of the 1970s (as illustrated in Table 2.3 on p. 8) were only an extreme form of the tendency during that decade for real post-tax returns to lenders to have been generally lower than in the two preceding decades – and far lower than in the 1920s and 1930s.

In any period when the problem is to check inflation it is dangerous to allow real post-tax returns on financial assets to fall to a level where people seek to hold larger stocks of real assets as alternatives – which tends to raise prices generally, as pointed out on pp. 30–2. But such a setting of monetary and tax policy means that the real returns to lenders are not as high as the real social returns that could be obtained (pre-tax) by investing in many investment projects that are not being undertaken; for there are virtually always potential investment projects available with a clearly positive social real return. These projects may well not be the ones that obtain the funds (whilst less promising ones are among those likely to obtain funds) when real post-tax returns to the lenders are kept artificially low by the monetary and tax policies prevailing. The policies in question also hold up the cost to the borrower to some extent by making it necessary to obtain a return on a project that is both high enough to enable the borrower to pay tax himself on the income, and also to pay a return to the lender that is high enough to persuade him to provide the funds after he has made appropriate provision to pay tax on the earnings. With these obstacles to the free flow of funds into potentially productive projects it is not surprising that capital markets operate very inefficiently and that investment and rates of productivity increase are low – as they were in the developed world generally in the 1970s.

It is probably significant that in the countries where macroeconomic problems were handled reasonably successfully in the 1970s – notably West Germany, and Austria (as also in Switzerland) – real post-tax returns to lenders were generally positive, or at least not so low as they were in most of the OECD countries, and that productivity rose relatively rapidly in those countries, despite a fairly high ratio of total tax to total output in them (by international standards).

It is thus important to emphasise that it is unlikely to be sufficient to ensure that real post-tax interest rates are merely positive. They probably need to approximate to the real return from those investment projects that are on the margin of being socially worthwhile. In any case, the existence of low or negative real post-tax interest rates is merely an indication that it is a defective mix of macroeconomic policies that is (partly or largely) responsible for stagflation. The overriding principle should be to cut tax rates so long as stagflation prevails, and to adopt a monetary policy that will restrain inflation, in the face of the tax cuts, in the process of restoring full employment.

Taxation and portfolio balance effects and prices

Low real returns to lenders are, then, likely to make them correspondingly more attracted towards *real* assets that are better hedges against inflation than are the alternative *financial* assets; and as the real assets in question are generally in relatively inelastic supply, this tends to raise the price level generally. The relative attractiveness of financial assets will be changed not only by rises and falls in pre-tax interest rates, but also by changes in rates of taxation on the earnings from the financial assets. This means that cuts in the taxes paid on the earnings from financial assets will tend to cause a shift in people's portfolios in the direction of a higher proportion of financial assets and a smaller proportion in value of those real assets that are held as alternatives to financial assets. Cuts in company or corporation taxes will also operate in the same direction by enabling the firms concerned to pay higher post-tax dividends, so that the holding of their shares becomes correspondingly more attractive. Reductions in other taxes paid by businesses – payroll tax, for example – also tend to increase profits after tax, and so the possibility of businesses paying higher returns on the financial claims against them held by lenders. If capital gains on financial assets are taxed, but those on alternative real assets – owner-occupied houses being an obvious example – are not taxed, a reduction in tax rates will make real assets seem correspondingly less attractive than when taxes were higher.

Indexed financial assets

The availability of index-linked financial assets (such as 'people's' bonds in Britain) or even long-term ones that have a rate linked to some short-term rate that varies with inflation, would make people more inclined to hold financial assets. Even without an actual change in the real rate of interest (as normally measured), as indexed assets remove some of the uncertainty about current real rates of return, which is an important element in causing people to seek to hold more real assets (and for the producers of exhaustible resources to avoid producing and selling them). The widespread introduction of index-linked assets would therefore reduce the 'risk premium' that erects a 'wedge' between the price that lenders require and that which borrowers will offer; and that would reduce nominal interest rates generally, whilst tending to reduce the price level.

The mix and the price of exhaustible resources

The adoption of a mix of measures that leaves the real post-tax return on financial assets low, or not sufficiently certain to constitute a good hedge against inflation, has the effect of making the owners of exhaustible resources, such as oil, more likely to keep it in the ground, or to demand correspondingly higher prices to persuade them to sell it. Economists considering the optimal rate of extraction for exhaustible resources such as minerals have generally pointed to the real rate of interest as one factor that has a bearing on how fast the owners ought to deplete such an asset. But it is only over the past decade or so that this has become an important matter for macroeconomic policy – though one that seems to have been neglected.

It is generally believed that the upward pressure on oil prices during the 1970s has been an important factor causing cost inflation and unemployment. The high price of oil has entered into the costs of many other items; it has acted like an indirect tax on consumers, by raising the costs of oil to them and consequently diverting expenditure from other items. Governments often reacted to oil price rises by trying to hold down the general level of activity, partly in the hope of thereby ensuring that the necessary reduction in real living standards was effected by restraint in wage increases (as well as in other incomes), and partly because they hoped that the consequently lower level of activity would hold down the volume of their oil purchases and consequently also check the rise in oil prices.

But the mix of measures with which they held back demand in the 1970s was generally one that kept real post-tax interest rates low, or even negative. It is not surprising, therefore, that the exporters of oil demanded high and rising prices for their oil to persuade them to export the desired quantity of it, in circumstances where it would have been better for them to keep much more of it in the ground as a hedge against inflation if oil prices had not risen so much. The mix of measures used to hold down activity in the oil-importing countries was thus one that tended to hold *up* world oil prices.

This means, however, merely that the mix chosen was one that tended to raise the *real* price of oil (in terms of other goods and services). The monetarist economists who point to the expansion of the quantity of money in the 1970s (much of it preceding the big rise in oil prices) as responsible for the high rate of inflation in the 1970s have much evidence in their favour.[3] In other words, the big rise in the *nominal*, as distinct from the *real*, price of oil could probably not have come about if there had not been such a rapid expansion of the quantity of money. But as the relatively low real post-tax return on financial assets during the 1970s resulted from measures of monetary policy (an 'easy monetary policy', both in the sense that a monetarist might use the term and also in the sense in which the term is used in this book) the rise in the *real* price of oil led to a large rise in its *nominal* price and also in the price level generally.

It is true that if other prices had been almost as flexible downwards as oil prices were upwards, this rise in the real price of oil need not have been accompanied by a large rise in the price level generally. If monetary policies had been less expansionary, and the mix of measures with which deflation had been applied had been one with a slower expansion of the quantity of money, the same upward adjustment of the real price of oil might well have been effected with a slower rise in the general price level. But in the modern world, prices (especially wage rates) generally are not very flexible downwards, and many governments were reluctant to put this matter fully to the test by tolerating a sharp fall in the real (and nominal) level of demand, which might then have meant a sharper rise in unemployment than actually occurred.

There is, however, some evidence that the governments that permitted a sharp contraction in demand (especially by way of a tight monetary policy) in the mid-1970s (Japan and West Germany, for example) recovered from both the cost-inflation due to the oil price rise, and then from the unemployment of the mid-1970s, more quickly than did some others (Britain, for example) that tried to sustain employment in this period in the face of the cost-push effect of the oil price rises. The fact remains, however, that a sharp rise in the price of such an important input item as oil is likely to have at least some upward effect on the general price level at a given level of activity, in a world where so many prices (most obviously the price of labour, wages) are not very flexible downwards. The point may be expressed by saying that such a rise means that governments are likely to have to tolerate a very sharp increase in unemployment if they hope to secure the required downward impact on other prices by this means. The main arguments put forward in this book stress that any such adjustment is made more difficult (that is, more likely to cause stagflation) if any given level of employment is established with relatively low real post-tax returns to lenders and relatively high tax rates (which was the mix used generally in the 1970s). It is because the elasticity of supply of substitutes for exhaustible resources is low that this relative price change leads to a rise in the average level of real costs – the amount of real resources needed to produce a given real

The Basic Proposals 39

output – when the supplies of the exhaustible resources that are put on the market (at any given price) are reduced.

Of course, oil is not the only exhaustible resource. All minerals come into this category, and so do those qualities of the soil that are used up in agriculture and in forestry (including deforestation). One might also argue that machinery is to some extent an exhaustible resource, so far as it is used up at all when it is being operated (that is, so far as it has a 'user cost'). People, too, can overwork themselves at one stage of their working week (or working life) and so reduce their ability to work at other times. But usually decisions about how much to work a machine or a human body are determined overwhelmingly by factors other than the available real returns on financial assets: for machinery, the rate of obsolescence is usually crucial; for human beings, the opportunities for work and leisure are of major importance – and, in any event, one seldom knows how far one's ability to work in future may be reduced (or enhanced) by working especially hard now.

In principle, however, when real rates of interest are low, the real price required to persuade the owner of an exhaustible resource to sell a given amount of it ought to be influenced by the real rate of return obtainable (after tax) from holding one of the available financial assets instead of retaining so much of the exhaustible resources. If a relatively low real rate of return on financial assets induces the producer to demand high real prices, this is likely to exert upward pressure on prices generally, since other prices (especially money wage rates) are relatively sticky downwards in the modern world. This is especially likely to be true if the mix in question is one that leaves the quantity of money rising relatively rapidly, as the result of insufficiently tight monetary measures being adopted. Both those who emphasise the cost-inflationary effect of oil price rises and also those who blame the excessive rise in the quantity of money for the inflation of the 1970s have a good deal of evidence to support their views. But merely to reduce the rise in the quantity of money by imposing even higher tax rates (which would have satisfied the monetarist aim of slowing down the rise in the quantity of money) would have made stagflation worse. It might also have tended to cause further rises in the real price of oil if it reduced the return available to oil producers on the financial (and real) assets that they purchased with the proceeds of their oil exports.

Conclusion on monetary policy

The main implication of the foregoing paragraphs is that the choice of a mix with a relatively expansionary monetary policy will exert an upward effect on prices, compared with one in which monetary policy is tighter and real interest rates are therefore higher. This means that a shift in the direction of a mix with tighter monetary policy will tend to have some downward effect on prices (compared with what they would otherwise have been); and that a policy that holds up unemployment whilst trying to reduce interest rates by monetary measures is likely to have less downward impact on the rise in prices over the period than one that operates with a tight monetary policy (and a correspondingly more expansionary budgetary policy).

GOVERNMENT SPENDING AND THE PRICE LEVEL

Most forms of government spending use resources without putting any additional goods and services on sale. If we compare two situations, each with the same level of employment, but one with a higher proportion of people (and other resources) being employed in producing government services, therefore, the amount of goods and services being sold on the market will be lower in this case than if the government sector was smaller and the output of marketable goods and services correspondingly greater.[4] The price level of marketable goods and services will therefore be higher in the former case – unless people decide to purchase correspondingly less by way of marketable goods and services simply because the government is producing more of them. They may, for example, purchase less by way of privately provided education services if the government provides them with free education; and if this occurs to a fully offsetting extent the larger size of the government sector would presumably not exert upward pressure on the price of education. But generally people do not reduce their total spending to an extent that fully offsets any free provision of certain goods and services by the government. Even if, in the example just given, they bought no privately provided education services at all, they would presumably feel able to purchase more of something else.

At the same time, some forms of government outlay help to hold down business costs. The provision of an efficient road system, for example, holds down costs generally; and one should not, therefore, assume that simply because a service is provided by the government it will necessarily tend to raise costs and prices; each form of government outlay has to be considered on its merits. Moreover, even if a reduction in a certain form of government spending (coupled with an offsetting rise in the production of goods and services for sale on the market) would tend to hold down prices, there may of course be other good arguments – social welfare or defence, for example –

to justify the outlays in question. But this does not affect the basic proposition that most forms of government outlay are such that a rise in the share of government spending usually tends to raise the price level at any given level of employment. If the higher level of government outlay is financed by higher taxes this will increase further the upward pressure on prices; if it is financed mainly by the sale of more bonds, there will be a counteracting effect on prices from this monetary measure.[5] (If it were financed by the creation of money this would be the most inflationary form of financing of all.)

COMBINING THE SWITCH WITH A STIMULUS

The greater the downward effect on price increases that the policy maker wishes to have in the immediate future, the greater should be both tax cuts and bond sales (or reductions in price-increasing forms of government spending) during the period in question. But the greater the extent to which the aim is to reduce unemployment, the greater should be the net stimulus applied. In other words, if a considerable real stimulus to employment is necessary, the tax cut must be relatively large by comparison with the bond sales.

If the view is taken that as unemployment starts to fall this will exert upward pressure on prices (and that is by no means certain when there is considerable spare capacity), the twist of mix in the appropriate direction would have to be correspondingly greater for any given real stimulus.

In short, then, the greater the change in the setting of the instruments (*at any given level of employment*) in the appropriate directions, the greater will be the price-restraining effect of the switch of mix (at that level of employment). At the same time, the greater the stimulus to employment that is to be applied, the more must taxes be cut *for any given bond sale, or for any given restraint in government spending.*

A non-inflationary stimulus

Policies that are intended to bring down inflation by tolerating high unemployment are sometimes defended by the assertion that *any* form of stimulus is bound to be inflationary. It is therefore worth outlining a policy to provide a stimulus in a way that can operate *only* so far as it exerts a downward pressure on the price level. Such a policy is always possible provided only that some forms of stimulus are more inflationary than others.

Provided that one accepts that tax cuts have some cost-reducing effects that are not shared by easy monetary policies (or by increases in government spending) having the same effect on employment; or if one believes that a move towards a mix with a tighter monetary policy, leading to higher real post-tax interest rates, exerts a downward impact on prices at a given level of activity, it is possible to raise the real quantity of money without an increase (and, indeed, even with some reduction) in the nominal quantity of money. The rise in the real quantity of money and in real disposable incomes that results from the downward impact on prices, and from the upward impact on real post-tax incomes, provides a (non-inflationary) stimulus to private expenditure.

The simplest case is where the loss of tax revenue that can normally be expected to result from a cut in tax rates would be exactly balanced by sales of securities to the non-bank public. The rise in the *real* stock of money (with a constant nominal stock), that results from the downward impact of both these measures on costs and prices, provides a stimulus so long as prices are in fact lower than they would otherwise have been. Indeed, a bond sale slightly larger than the loss of tax revenue could still leave the real stock of money (and disposable incomes) higher in the face of the fall in costs, despite the fall in the *nominal* value of the quantity of money. (The rise in the rate of interest that may follow the suggested measures, at least temporarily, may also tend to raise the velocity of circulation, and so nominal incomes; but this does not alter the fact that the price reductions provide a non-inflationary stimulus.)

On the other hand, even if bond sales were made to a slightly *lower* value than the cut in tax revenue (the nominal quantity of money thus rising), the net effect could still be the provision of some price-reducing stimulus. For example, if the switch of mix reduced the price level at a given level of activity by, say, 2 per cent, a rise in the nominal quantity of money by anything less than 2 per cent would provide a price-reducing stimulus (if the velocity of circulation – and so the amount of money that people wanted to hold at a given money income – were constant). If the rise in the real level of activity itself affected the price level (upwards or downwards) this would also have to be taken into account. But the main reason why people (including those who assert that *all* stimuluses *must* be inflationary) expect recovery to be accompanied by price rises is not that rising activity of itself necessarily causes rises in prices, but simply because in the past the forms of stimulus usually employed have consisted predominantly of *easier* monetary policies, higher government spending, and tax cuts that initially stimulate consumption – which operate mainly by a process that tends to raise the price level. The use of a price-reducing form of stimulus would thus not necessarily have any upward effect on prices as unemployment fell.

The main reason why such forms of stimulus have not been tried in the

The Basic Proposals 43

past (so far as the writer is aware) is presumably that a tax cut *alone*, financed by creating money, would be much more attractive politically – and that would almost invariably exert an *upward* impact on prices; whereas the essential concomitant for a *non-inflationary* stimulus – selling more bonds to the public on about the same scale as the reduction in tax revenue – is likely to *appear* to be a strange policy to adopt for overcoming a recession (even in harness with a tax cut). Normally, therefore, the easy and attractive part of such a mix – the tax cut – is likely to be tried – but (as in Finland, Canada, Ireland, Denmark and Britain at various times in the 1970s) it is normally likely to be accompanied by *easier* monetary policies and *higher* government spending. The incorrect conclusion is then likely to be drawn that *all* stimulatory policies *must* be inflationary – simply because the forms that operate by price reductions (a more inflationary form of stimulus being reduced and a less inflationary one being increased) have not (apparently) been widely employed – if ever.

DOES IT MATTER IF TAX CUTS DO NOT RAISE EMPLOYMENT?

Various arguments have been raised in support of the view that tax cuts may not lead to a reduction in unemployment even in a recession. This is highly unlikely ever to be true; but if it were true, so far from constituting an objection to one of the mixes involving tax cuts, it would constitute an especially favourable situation for using one of those mixes to cure stagflation. The less a tax cut stimulates employment, the more it will reduce inflation.

A tax cut financed by the sale of additional bonds to the non-bank public might not constitute a stimulus, because the downward effect of the bond sales on employment might offset the upward effects of the tax cut. It has not been proposed above that the tax cuts should necessarily be offset exactly (in terms of their monetary effect) by additional bond sales; the additional sale of bonds required to hold activity constant might be more than, or less than, or the same as, whatever reduction in revenue resulted from the tax cut (or, indeed, bond *purchases* might actually have to be made by the government if revenue *rose* as a result of the cuts in tax rates). The greater the depressing effect of any bond sales, the less would the sale of bonds need to be to maintain employment constant – or, of course, to bring about any desired upward (or downward) effect on the level of employment. (Discussions of bond-financed tax cuts usually assume implicitly that the aim is to maintain a constant level, or rate of increase, in the *quantity of money* in face of the tax cuts. In fact, however, if the tax cut has any cost-reducing effects, a *constant* nominal quantity of money would provide a *real stimulus*.) Another argument is that businesses and consumers might be so concerned by the rise in the budget deficit that they could be expected to reduce their own expenditure to an extent that would equal or exceed the upward effect on spending that would normally result from the rise in disposable incomes (at any given pre-tax income) brought about by the tax cut. It is virtually inconceivable that this could occur; but one could not rule it out as a theoretical possibility. It must, however, be considered as such a remote possibility that it could never reasonably be considered a sound basis for policy.

If a tax cut did not result in any stimulus to employment this would mean that the tax cuts were having no demand-inflationary effects to set against their cost-reducing effects. In other words, the less a tax cut adds to total demand, and the more any offsetting monetary measures tend to depress demand, the greater the extent to which the cost-reducing effects of the switch of mix in question will exceed any demand-inflationary effects of the tax cut. This is clearly a highly promising situation in which to adopt such a mix. Even if taxes had relatively little cost-inflationary effects, provided that tax cuts had little or no demand-expansionary effect (or, better still, if they should actually *depress* demand – perhaps because businessmen were intensely worried by a resulting rise in the budget deficit) a given switch of mix in these directions would have a correspondingly greater downward effect on costs and prices at any given level of activity.

In other words, if tax cuts did not stimulate employment the taxes in question would have been quite indefensible – for the taxes would not be restraining private demand, and could therefore have had only *adverse* effects – by reducing productivity through the resources diverted to administering them (and perhaps to evading and avoiding them), and through all the other channels by which any tax normally worsens the allocation of resources. Any such tax should certainly be scrapped. The fact that they are *not* scrapped by politicians and economic advisers, even those who have publicly expressed the view that tax cuts actually *increase* unemployment, suggests either that the view is not sincerely held, or that the long habit of thinking of tax cuts as a stimulus to employment – rather than, as they should be in a situation of stagflation, as primarily a cure for cost-inflation – dies very hard indeed.

Indeed, if tax cuts had no demand-expansionary effects, politicians would be faced with not merely the possibility, but the duty, of curing stagflation by a combination of tax cuts, lower interest rates, and consequently lower unemployment and lower inflation: and no politician could have a more wonderful dream than that.

The Basic Proposals 45

STIMULATING CONSUMPTION OR PRODUCTION?

If a government tries to increase employment by raising either consumers' demand or its own demand for goods and services, it is likely to exert a greater immediate upward effect on prices than if the same stimulus to employment were provided initially and directly to production, by reducing the various forms of tax paid by firms (or by subsidies in forms that reduced business costs generally). Standard (Keynesian) analysis ignores this point, taking it for granted – at least implicitly – that when there are unused resources, *any* form of stimulus is equally likely to bring them into production, without the choice of stimulus making any difference to whatever effects there may be on the price level. This was presumably a reasonable approach in the 1930s, when inflation was not a problem; but it is definitely not a suitable approach to policy in a situation of stagflation.

The issue is of considerable significance partly because governments seem so often in the past to have provided a stimulus mainly by increases in their own demands for goods and services, or by increases in social-services benefits, or by cuts in the (direct or indirect) taxes paid by consumers, all of which exert their initial impact on demand by increasing spending before any extra production of goods and services comes on to the market to meet these extra demands. Presumably it has usually been more attractive politically to make budgetary concessions in these forms – which are immediately apparent to the taxpayer, to the social services beneficiary, or to the producer of goods and services for the government (including those employed by the government) – than are reductions in taxes paid by employers, which can be represented by political opponents as 'giving away money to business'.

The essential difference between a tax cut that provides the stimulus by initially increasing demand and one that does so by reducing costs of production is that the latter is likely to exert most or all of its impact on demand more or less simultaneously with a decision to increase production. For the extra people employed are simultaneously producing goods and services that will come on the market almost at once. By contrast, a stimulus to consumption demand, or government spending on goods and services, does nothing to increase initially the output of the consumption goods that will be purchased out of the extra incomes thus created. Of course, *in both cases* there will usually be indirect effects upon the supplies of consumption goods and services, as producers react to the additional demand for their products by producing more of them. But the extra incomes created in those industries then also lead to a further rise in consumer demand. There is thus no reason to expect the *indirect* repercussions to be any different if the *initial* impact is by way of those types of tax cuts (or government spending) that raise *demand* initially from what it would be if it was provided by way of the types of tax cuts that reduce costs of production. But the *direct* effects are different, provided that producers react *to some extent* by increasing their output when their costs are reduced by tax cuts, so that the extra consumer demand is to that extent offset by the immediate additional production of goods and services to meet it.

If tax cuts are such that the producers benefit only to the extent that they increase their output (as they would if the tax cuts or subsidies were available to them only so far as they increased their production), this effect would be maximised. But that sort of tax cut is seldom practicable. Any reductions in business costs resulting from cuts in taxes paid by producers are, however, likely to lead to *some* rise in real output prior to, or virtually simultaneous with, any consequent rise in expenditure.

This is not to deny that some of the tax concessions to business might simply go to swell the profits and the consumption of the owners of the businesses and their shareholders; and so far as that was true the stimulus to demand and output would occur only as they subsequently spent the higher incomes. To that extent, the effects on prices and real output of the stimulus in question would be no different from those of a reduction in taxes on consumption or on personal incomes, or those of a rise in pensions. But any tax cut that tends to reduce producers' costs will presumably stimulate output (at a given price level) to some extent, or else hold down prices (at a given output); and either of these effects is desirable in a situation of stagflation.

One implication of this is that every time a government tries to increase taxes that impinge on business costs (rather than on consumption), this tends to make stagflation worse; for it makes unemployment likely to rise (at any given price level) and prices likely to be higher at any given level of output or employment. On the other hand, if the same amount of tax revenue were raised in ways that tended to hold down consumption initially, the shift from taxation of business to taxation of consumption could reduce the upward pressure on prices at any given level of employment. It should, however, be borne in mind that high taxes on consumers may have upward effects *on money wage increases*, and that this may indirectly increase business costs, and to that extent operate somewhat like a tax on business costs. For so far as wage and salary-earners take account of taxation in deciding their wage demands, reductions in these forms of taxes can restrain increases in wages, which are a major element in business costs. But this effect – though potentially important – is not likely to reflect *fully* and immediately any cut in taxation. The greatest reduction in business costs (for a given fall in tax revenue) is thus likely to be a cut in the taxes paid by businesses on their inputs (including taxes on their wage bill). In a situation of stagflation, therefore, generally the taxes that it is initially most helpful to reduce are those paid by businesses.

It is not surprising that governments have failed to distinguish those forms of stimulus that operate by reducing costs from those that operate by initially increasing demand and prices; for economists have almost always failed to differentiate between those different types of stimulus on these grounds, as there has been no widely accepted criterion to favour some forms of stimulus as being non-inflationary (or, at least, *less* inflationary) than others. This seems to have led to *all* forms of stimulus being given a bad name in some official and business circles (and also among many economists).

Interest rate reductions and business costs

Clearly, interest rates are one important cost of business, and one can therefore understand businesses asking for a stimulus to be given by way of reductions in interest rates. But an easier monetary policy also has its initial effect to some considerable extent by providing a stimulus to spending – especially in countries where a high proportion of consumption is financed by some form of borrowing (such as hire purchase). (An easing of monetary policy also has the effect of raising the nominal values of bonds, and real estate; and this may also give a stimulus to additional consumption by their owners.) That effect acts like the demand stimulus provided by a reduction in the taxes paid by consumers, but its initial impact operates by raising the price level, and before long also the actual and expected rate of inflation. In this important sense, therefore, a stimulus to total demand provided by way of an easy monetary policy is more likely to raise consumption and prices than is the same stimulus to demand provided by cuts in the taxes paid by productive enterprises. So far as it stimulates investment outlays – rather than additional output from existing capital goods – that also has an immediate upward effect on prices; though the extra investment will eventually give rise to additional real output of finished goods.

The failure of economists to distinguish in these respects between these different types of stimuli is typified in the frequent use of the phrase 'expansion of demand' as a synonym for an 'expansion of employment' or 'activity'. It is therefore important to emphasise that a given stimulus to total *demand* may have more or less effect in stimulating *employment* (and real *output*) according to whether it is given mainly in ways that encourage spending (when much of its effect may be to raise *prices*) or mainly in ways that more or less immediately encourage *production* and *employment* (as well as the consumption of those who consequently become employed). As the *form* in which a stimulus to *demand* is provided is thus an important determinant of the extent to which it will also be a stimulus to *employment*, the two words should not be used synonymously to mean *any* form of expansion of total spending in the economy.

SHOULD TAXES BE HIGH WHEN GOVERNMENT SPENDING IS HIGH?

We have so far adopted the approach of considering the effect of varying the setting of pairs of the broad groups of macroeconomic instruments while keeping the other at a given setting. But this approach is purely an expository one; for in fact any government ought to vary all its instruments together in such a way as to achieve the best approximation it can to the macroeconomic aims that it has in view.

This means that if it chooses a relatively high ratio of government spending to total output, any given level of employment must be achieved with *either* higher tax rates *or* a tighter monetary policy (or some combination of the two) than would have been appropriate if government spending had been at a lower ratio to total output. If the government wishes to minimise the upward pressure on the price level that is likely to be associated with a relatively high ratio of government spending to total output, it ought to choose to offset the upward pressure on prices solely or mainly by keeping monetary policy relatively tight (for that will exert some downward pressure on prices) rather than by raising tax rates (for that would add to cost inflation). (Similarly, every easing of monetary policy and every rise in tax rates makes it harder to stop stagflation.)

The implication of this flies in the face of the generally accepted wisdom about the need to keep taxes high when government spending is high. For the implication is that if a government chooses to keep price-increasing forms of government spending relatively high, it should aim to keep tax rates relatively low (provided that monetary policy is kept correspondingly tighter); so that it ought, on this criterion, to run a relatively *larger* budget deficit (at any given level of activity) when these forms of government spending are *high* than when they are low (relative to total output). Yet in fact governments often argue that they have been unable to reduce tax rates because it has proved difficult or impossible to curtail government spending. In contrast to this view, the implication of the present argument is that the relatively high level of government spending makes it especially important to exert more downward pressure on costs by reducing tax rates (and keeping monetary policy correpondingly tighter) if the aim is to minimise the upward pressure of the high level of government spending on prices (at any given level of activity).

It remains true, however, that the overall setting of monetary policy and taxation *taken together* must be made correspondingly more contractionary if government spending is at a relatively high level. But so long as there is inflation at less than full employment it will always be appropriate to reduce tax rates: and only if a sufficient tightening of monetary policy to offset the demand effects of the relatively high level of government spending was more than sufficient to offset any price-increasing effects of the government spending would it be safe to increase tax rates (from the point of view of preventing a rise in prices). The precise combination of measures required clearly depends on their relative effects on the price level for a given effect on employment. But at any given level of employment, the presumption is that taxes should be kept relatively *low* (and monetary policy correspondingly tighter) when governement spending is relatively *high*. By contrast, the usual presumption of most governments is that there should be a more or less equal rise in tax revenue to balance a given rise in government spending – in effect a commitment to maintain a particular figure for the budget surplus or deficit. But if they operate on that principle they are likely to make stagflation worse than it need be, with any given level of government spending; for such an approach will lead them mainly to raise tax rates rather than to tighten monetary policy when government spending is raised.

HOW MUCH SHOULD EACH INSTRUMENT BE VARIED?

The foregoing discussion has emphasised that the relative effects of the principal macroeconomic instruments upon prices and employment (respectively) are relevant for deciding the direction in which the setting of each of them should be changed in a situation of stagflation. If instrument A has less upward (or a greater downward) effect on prices than does instrument B, for a given effect in reducing unemployment, instrument A should be moved in a more expansionary direction, and instrument B in a less expansionary (or more contractionary) direction than would otherwise have been appropriate. The extent to which the setting of a particular instrument should be changed depends on how much a given change in it will reduce unemployment and how much it will affect the price level.

Questions that have often been discussed in the past about the relative effect of different instruments on the general level of demand have therefore to be replaced in a situation of stagflation by questions about their respective impacts on prices compared with those on employment. It is sometimes argued that a particular change in one of these instruments is likely to have little effect on employment. But, provided there is some difference between the relative effects of at least two of the available instruments on prices and employment (respectively), there is in principle a mix that will reduce stagflation. The actual size of the relative effects of each instrument on employment determines only the *size* of the change in each instrument that will be required in order to have a given effect.

For example, if the mix under discussion is a tax cut coupled with a tightening of monetary policy (on whatever scale is necessary in order to keep activity at some desired level) it is no objection to such a proposal to advance the view that a given level of bond sales will have a relatively small effect (or, conversely, a relatively large effect) on employment; for such considerations affect only the extent of the bond sales that would be required in order to offset the employment effects of a given tax cut. If a tightening of monetary policy (typified by a given sale of bonds) has a relatively large effect in holding down employment (that is, there is much 'crowding out') this merely means that a correspondingly smaller tightening of monetary policy will be required for any given tax cut.

Or if the view is taken that a tax cut has relatively little upward effect on employment, this would merely mean that tax cuts could and should be correspondingly larger for any given bond sale. Monetary policy would then not need to be tightened as much for any given tax cut as on the opposite assumption. (If one wished to make the very far-fetched assumption that tax cuts actually *increased* unemployment, this would imply the need to *ease* monetary policy when taxes were cut.)

To take another example, if a tightening of monetary policy has relatively little effect in restraining demand, a given tax cut would need to be accompanied by a correspondingly more severe tightening of monetary policy.

To summarise the foregoing paragraphs, the more a given tax cut stimulates employment, the tighter must be the setting of monetary policy (in order to establish a given level of employment): whilst the less any given tightening of monetary policy does to restrain demand, the more it will need to be tightened in order to balance the effect of a given tax cut.

A view near to what is usually called the 'Keynesian' end of the spectrum would be that investment spending is not very sensitive to changes in monetary policy, but that many forms of spending react relatively strongly to budgetary policy. If this is so, it would be necessary to make relatively large changes in the setting of monetary policy in order to balance the effects on employment of a given change in the setting of a budgetary instrument.

On the other hand, the implication of a 'monetarist' view, to the effect that private spending is likely to react relatively strongly to changes in the setting of monetary policy, but not to changes in budgetary policy, would be that only a small tightening of monetary policy would be required in order to offset the effects of a given tax cut. With such assumptions as these, one would make relatively large tax cuts and accompany them with a relatively slight tightening of monetary policy in a situation of stagflation.

There is nothing paradoxical in arguing that someone starting from *monetarist* assumptions ought to favour relatively large changes in *budgetary* policy (and vice versa) in a situation of stagflation. If there appears to be a paradox it is simply because the argument between these views has in the past been merely about their respective effects on *total* income or employment, whereas the present discussion bears on their respective contributions to stopping stagflation (through their differential effects on prices and on employment).

If one applies the above principles to the mix that involves reducing the ratios of both taxation and government spending to total output as a means of checking stagflation, the implication would be that if a given tax cut has a relatively large effect in increasing employment, the accompanying restraint in government spending would have to be correspondingly greater. On the other hand, if a large proportion of a given tax cut is saved by the taxpayers, the reduction in the share of government spending to total output (for any given tax cut) would not have to be as large. If a reduction in government spending is likely to have considerable *adverse* effects on private investment – as most non-monetarist economists would say was likely during a recession – a relatively large tax cut would be needed to balance a given fall in government spending. But if government spending had been 'crowding out' private investment, large cuts in government spending could, and should, be made for any given tax cut.

If the mix of higher government spending and tight monetary policy was being applied, a Keynesian would argue that the rise in government spending would have a relatively large effect in reducing unemployment, and would thus need to be balanced by a correspondingly greater tightening of monetary policy. On the other hand, a monetarist would presumably not expect the rise in government spending to do much to raise the overall level of employment, and would therefore not expect that it would need to be balanced to any great extent by a tightening of monetary policy.

SUMMARY OF MAIN ARGUMENT

If taxes have cost-inflationary effects that are not shared by cuts in government spending or by tight monetary measures having the same effect on employment, tax cuts coupled with either a tighter monetary policy or lower government outlays can exert at least some once-for-all downward impact on the price level over some period at a given level of employment. If this switch of mix is combined with the provision of a net real stimulus – for example by a bond-financed tax cut, operating through a fall in the price level and a consequent rise in the real quantity of money – a non-inflationary stimulus is possible.

If tighter monetary policies, or reductions in many forms of government spending, also have price-reducing effects (apart from any that operate through the real level of demand) this argument becomes correspondingly stronger. If a switch of mix could achieve the same sort of slowing down in the rise in prices over the period in question as the government is hoping to achieve by tolerating temporarily high unemployment, it is clearly socially costly and unnecessary to use high unemployment for this purpose. At any rate, one would have to provide convincing economic arguments for the view that all of the possible switches of mix would have social costs in excess of those resulting from tolerating temporarily high unemployment (even on the assumption that the latter policy would in fact succeed in reducing inflation). Moreover, the possibility of unemployment achieving the desired effects on inflation over the period in question depends partly on the mix of measures with which the deflation is carried out. If the unemployment was achieved with a mix that included a very expansionary monetary policy and high tax rates, such a policy could make inflation worse, even if the rise in unemployment was in itself tending to hold down inflation.

4 Balance of Payments Aspects

The mixes suggested in the preceding chapter for reducing the upward pressure on prices at any given level of activity will also thereby improve a country's competitive position at any given exchange rate, or tend to cause the exchange rate to appreciate if it is free to do so. This is partly because of the downward pressure on prices that a shift of mix in one of these directions exerts over the period in which it is introduced. But, in addition, the mix that involves a tightening of monetary policy and lower taxes tends to improve the capital account of the balance of payments, at least in the immediate future; though this may be expected eventually to lead to a greater outflow (or a smaller inflow) of interest and dividends, which will at that future time make the balance of payments or the exchange rate to that extent weaker than it would have been (at the same level of activity) if the change of mix had not occurred. The mix involving higher government spending and tighter monetary policy may be expected to have similar effects on the capital account, and so on future flows of interest and dividends; whilst the effect on the capital account of that involving reductions in both tax revenue and government spending (as a proportion of GDP) is uncertain.

If an appropriate shift of mix is combined with a net stimulus, therefore, the shift would tend to offset the weakening of the exchange rate (or the movement of the balance of payments in the direction of deficit) that could otherwise be expected to result from a stimulus to activity. A sufficient twist of the mix in an appropriate direction could thus, in principle, prevent an expansionary policy from leading to a weakening of the exchange rate; and a smaller shift of the mix in the right direction would moderate the depreciation (and consequent inflation) associated with a given real stimulus. This would clearly be desirable, even for a country with adequate reserves, so long as it is worried about inflation.

One way of viewing these effects is to consider them as operating through changes in people's demands for money balances (the so-called 'monetary' or 'portfolio' approach to the balance of payments). If a stimulus is given mainly by an expansionary budget, with monetary policy kept relatively tight, this will lead people to try to build up their cash balances to a more adequate level by borrowing more (and lending less) overseas, and by making greater efforts to sell more and buy less – which tends to improve a country's current account. Both these effects strengthen the exchange rate (at any given level of employment) by comparison with a stimulus that mainly takes the form of an expansionary monetary policy. This therefore means that a monetary stimulus will cause more upward pressure on the price level, by causing more depreciation – as well as through the (closed economy) channels discussed in the preceding chapter – at any given level of employment. The greater the use of monetary measures of expansion, therefore, and the less taxes are reduced, the more will any given real stimulus lead to depreciation and inflation, and the more unemployment is thus likely to be needed (or, at least, tolerated) in the hope of holding down inflation over the relevant period. (The operation of appropriate policy mixes in an open economy is discussed in more detail elsewhere: see Perkins, 1979, Chapters 5 and 6.)[1]

The present chapter considers a number of balance-of-payments aspects of the use of the policy mix to deal with macroeconomic problems that are of topical importance in the early 1980s. We shall look first at the question of dealing with stagflation in an open economy from the viewpoint of the country applying the policy; and then consider whether the proposed policy can reasonably be said to be likely to have adverse effects on the rest of the world.

THE MIX AND INTERNATIONAL COMPETITIVENESS

A country's international competitiveness depends on the exchange rate and on movements in its price level (together with its competitiveness in non-price factors, such as advertising and distribution). The combination of macroeconomic measures with which any given level of employment is established will affect both movements in a country's price level (relative to that of the rest of the world) and the exchange rate.

If the mix of measures that a country chooses is one that tends to hold down prices – low taxes and a tight monetary policy, in particular – its industries will be more competitive at any given exchange rate than they would be with the opposite setting of these instruments. At the same time, if a tight money mix leads to a stronger capital account than one with an easier monetary policy (as is likely) the exchange rate will be stronger; and, to that extent, while the extra capital inflow is occurring, the international competitiveness of the industries of the country concerned will be *less at any given relative price level* than if it had a mix with an easier monetary policy. *But the appreciation itself will tend to hold down the price level in the country with the appreciating currency.*

If a country adopts an expansionary macroeconomic policy, the rise in output and employment will (in themselves) normally tend to cause a depreciation of its currency, by increasing the level of its imports (at any given exchange rate and relative price levels). But the greater the extent to which the stimulus is given by way of tax cuts coupled with a relatively tight monetary policy, the less will be the depreciation (or the greater the appreciation, if this choice of measures is carried far enough).

In principle, a fiscal expansion could be complemented by a monetary policy that was just sufficiently expansionary to hold relative interest rates constant between the home country and the rest of the world. Depreciation would then be likely to occur as a result of the higher level of activity (though that effect would be partly offset by any rise in capital inflow that resulted from the domestic expansion and from the consequently greater profitability of industry, and by any net reduction in cost inflation that resulted from the tax cuts). If the country in question was already enjoying as high a level of capital inflow as it felt to be in its long-run interests it might wish (from this point of view) to see interest rates held down by the choice of mix that relied largely on expansionary monetary measures. But if it did so it would find it correspondingly harder to reconcile any expansionary measures with price stability, as the balance of payments would be weaker and the exchange rate therefore more likely to depreciate than with the opposite mix. It seems unlikely that the level of capital inflow that would maximise its output in the long run would differ from that which would be appropriate from a macro point of view in the long run. But in the short run the ideal level of capital inflow might well be higher, from the macro point of view, than it would in the long run.

At the other extreme, the stimulus might rely so much on tax cuts coupled with tight monetary policy that the exchange rate did not depreciate at all (during the period when this policy increased capital inflow). But, even without any depreciation, the competitive position of the country's exporting and import-replacing industries (at any given level of employment) would still be improved as a result of the cost reductions, compared with their initial situation; though the relative stimulus given to other ('non-traded goods') industries would be greater in this case than if the chosen stimulus had relied to a greater extent on an easy monetary policy and less on tax cuts.

The greater the sensitivity of capital flows to changes in relative interest rates, the less would it be necessary to tighten monetary policy in order to have a given favourable effect on capital flows (and so on the exchange rate). Similarly, in such a situation, failure to keep monetary policy tight in the face of an expansionary budgetary policy would have a less favourable effect on capital inflow than would an expansionary policy that kept monetary policy relatively tight. If capital flows respond mainly to nominal interest rates (at least in the short run) a country that has an especially high rate of inflation, and which is therefore keeping monetary policy tight, will be able to attract considerable flows of capital by choosing a mix in which monetary policy is kept somewhat tighter; and, by the same token, if it gives way to domestic pressure to give more of the stimulus by easing monetary measures, the resulting fall in nominal interest rates (compared with the alternative policy) will make capital inflow correspondingly less, and depreciation and inflation therefore greater.

NOMINAL INTEREST RATES AND CAPITAL FLOWS

It has appeared likely in recent years that very high nominal interest rates can sometimes attract capital flows on a large scale even into countries with high rates of inflation (such as Britain in 1979–80) and away from countries where interest rates are low in nominal terms, even though they may be high there relative to the rate of inflation (as with West Germany in 1980).

This suggests that the owners of capital that can be fairly readily withdrawn from a country are not particularly concerned about the long-term prospects for its exchange rate (for the pound sterling was probably widely thought of as over-valued and the German mark as undervalued in 1979–80); and this is a reasonable view to take if the financial assets in which they are investing are ones that can be readily cashed, and the proceeds repatriated, if the expectation of an unfavourable exchange rate movement starts to be fulfilled.

If this attitude is typical – at least towards countries with well developed capital markets, in which financial assets can be readily sold, and from which the absence of exchange control on outward capital movements makes repatriation feasible – this means that a mix of measures operating through a tight monetary policy and high nominal rates of interest can have a relatively large effect in improving the capital account, even without the need to pay high *real* rates of interest. For it will be the countries with the highest rates of inflation that would be most likely to raise their nominal interest rates to high levels; and they may therefore attract capital inflows (or reduce net outflows) even when the *real* rates of interest in terms of their own rates of inflation are low.

MONETARY POLICY AND THE EXCHANGE RATE

It follows from what has been said above that the use of an easier monetary policy explicitly to weaken an exchange rate is not appropriate in a situation where a country is trying to restrain inflation. The advocates of an easier monetary policy – rather than tax cuts – in Britain in 1980–1 thought it desirable to improve the competitive position of British industry by causing the exchange rate to depreciate. Yet (when there is stagflation) the worst way to try to provide a stimulus, even if the exchange rate is thought to be 'over-valued', is to ease monetary policy (especially, if it is accompanied by an actual raising of tax rates, as it was in Britain in 1981); for the easing of monetary policy tends to raise prices by more than does a comparable stimulus to employment given by way of tax cuts. Indeed, it may not improve the competitive position of the country's industry at all, as any depreciation may be offset by the consequent upward pressure on prices; and even so far as an effective depreciation (a change in the exchange rate greater than the consequent price rise) does occur it will be accompanied by additional (and unnecessary) inflation; whereas the same stimulus brought about by tax cuts would have brought less upward pressure on the price level.

Moreover, a stimulus by way of tax cuts does not need to be accompanied by an effective depreciation in order to assist the country's industry. Even if a net stimulus provided by means of a tax cut (coupled with a tight monetary policy) left the exchange rate unchanged, a direct stimulus would still be given to industry by the tax cut itself. Any form of stimulus will tend to cause some depreciation, and the switch of mix towards lower tax rates (with a relatively tight monetary policy) would normally offset this only partly; so that some depreciation could be expected to result. But a depreciation effected in this way would be accompanied by *reductions* in costs (at each level of employment) as a result of the choice of this mix. It would thus be likely to result in a greater improvement in the competitive position of the country's industry than would have resulted if the same depreciation had been caused by means of an easier monetary policy.

Of course, if the alternative of easing monetary policy were accompanied by a net tightening of the overall setting of policy – as in the British budget of 1981 – the downward pressure of demand would be tending to cause more *appreciation*. To that extent the competitive position of the country's industry would therefore actually be worsened, as it would be also by the upward pressure on prices resulting from the choice of an easy money mix. A prescription for the worst possible result is thus a net tightening of the overall setting of policy – causing higher unemployment – coupled with a twist of mix towards reducing interest rates by an easing of monetary policy (and to that extent higher prices) and higher tax rates.

If the country's reserves are unnecessarily high, the combination of measures chosen should be one that will reduce them; whereas a depreciation would make it less likely that the excessively high reserves will be reduced. But if the reserves are high, this makes it possible to have a more expansionary policy than might otherwise have been thought possible, without the need for a depreciation and the consequent upward effect on prices. It is thus particularly indefensible for a country with high reserves to try to use devaluation as a stimulus: for it should be providing the stimulus by a mix of measures that *minimises* any consequent depreciation, thus making it more likely that the excessive reserves would be used up as a result of the movement towards external deficit that was associated with the stimulus. On the other hand, a country with *low* reserves and a *weak* balance of payments should be seeking to provide any desired stimulus in a way that would weaken its balance of payments little, if at all, but accepting whatever depreciation is inevitable, rather than drawing further on its inadequate reserves.

Even a country whose balance of payments is at present strong may have a case for building up its reserves (or other overseas investments) to a higher level – which would tend to cause its currency to depreciate. For example, there may have been a case for Britain to build up her reserves to a higher level in the first half of the 1980s against the time when North Sea oil would cease to save the country so much foreign exchange. But, if so, this case should be argued on its own merits. The argument should not be that official intervention to build up Britain's overseas reserves (or other overseas investments) should be undertaken on the grounds that the consequently weaker exchange rate would help British industry; for there are much less inflationary ways of assisting British industries (or those among them that are most adversely affected by the strong exchange rate).

EFFECTS OF A SWITCH OF MIX ON THE ALLOCATION OF RESOURCES IN AN OPEN ECONOMY

A switch of mix towards a tighter monetary policy and an easier budgetary policy in an open economy has sometimes been objected to on the grounds that the consequent appreciation of the currency (at least in the shorter run) will have an undesirable effect on the allocation of the country's resources among different industries, by adversely affecting 'traded goods' industries – those that export and those that compete most closely with imports.

But this effect would not be a valid objection to the proposed mix unless the social costs of any consequent unfavourable effects on traded goods industries exceeded the social benefits that would result from the higher level of activity in the economy that was the consequence of using the switch of mix (rather than a temporarily high level of unemployment) to restrain inflation – and there is no reason to think that is likely (or even possible, especially when the alternative would be a high level of unemployment).

The first point to emphasise is that the switch of mix would *not* operate purely by bringing about an appreciation. For if the tightening of monetary policy were accompanied by a lower level of tax rates than would otherwise have been possible, the competitive position of the traded goods industries would be consequently stronger than with the opposite mix (at any given level of employment and of the exchange rate). If, however, the tighter monetary policy were accompanied by a higher level of government spending (rather than lower tax rates) than would otherwise have been feasible, it is much less likely that the competitive position of the traded goods industries would have been improved by the switch of mix, as most forms of government spending probably tend to raise the price level at any given level of employment (whereas most forms of tax cuts tend to reduce it). But even in this case it is possible that the downward impact on prices of the tightening of monetary policy would have some favourable effect on the competitive position of traded goods industries; and some forms of government outlay may also operate in that direction (especially subsidies that hold down costs – which might be directed mainly towards traded goods industries, or towards those industries, whether 'traded' goods or not, whose long-run competitive position is believed to depend greatly on a healthy growth in the near future).

Let us now consider those effects of a switch of mix that operate *only* by strengthening the exchange rate, and thus weaken the international competitive position of traded goods industries. So far as the switch of mix in question enables the economy to operate at a higher level of real output than the government would have chosen in the absence of the switch of mix, this means that the traded goods industries, as well as many others, will be able to operate at a higher level of output, and that there will be a consequently greater incentive to businesses to undertake productive investment. This will be a factor tending to improve the country's competitive position in future.

Moreover, the appreciation that results from the rise in capital inflow caused by the choice of this mix will be only temporary; for it will eventually be equalled or exceeded by a movement of the exchange rate in the other direction, as interest payments, and perhaps repayments of capital, come to exceed any remaining net addition to capital inflow that results from the switch of mix. So far as those making investment decisions foresee these medium-run or longer-run developments, this will constitute a net stimulus to investment in traded goods industries (which will later consequently become more competitive) even in the short run; and it will provide a much greater stimulus in the longer run. If, however, those making investment decisions have shorter-run horizons than this, the switch of mix will give less incentive to traded goods than to non-traded goods industries in the short run. But the particular range of industries that should be designated as 'traded goods industries' will be constantly varying over time, and one cannot foresee with accuracy which industries will be most accurately described as 'traded' or 'non-traded' in future; so that it seems inappropriate to base one's current macroeconomic policy on the aim of giving most encouragement to *all* those industries that happen *at present* to be best able to export or to compete with imports. In any case, so far as the government can foresee which industries can justifiably be given any special assistance on grounds of long-run national interest, they should be given this assistance explicitly – rather than merely incidentally, along with all the other industries that are favoured by keeping monetary policy easy and taxes relatively high. Moreover, the stimulus to protectionism and to the toleration of high unemployment that results from the use of an inflationary mix seems certain to do far more harm to the allocation of resources than would a policy of full employment achieved with a low-tax, tight-money mix.[2]

STIMULATING EXPENDITURE OR PRODUCTION IN AN OPEN ECONOMY

It was pointed out in the previous chapter (pp. 45–7) that a stimulus to employment given by way of general subsidy or tax cut may have less upward effect on prices (or more downward effect on them) if it is in a form that reduces costs of production, and is thus likely to stimulate output at the same time as employment – rather than by way of a stimulus to expenditure at the first instance. For a stimulus to expenditure may be expected to cause an upward pressure on demand for goods and services which is not initially offset (even partly) by extra production. (It was pointed out that the subsequent indirect effects on output – assuming that there is spare capacity – may be assumed to be broadly the same for either type of stimulus; this means that the net difference between them remains the initial upward pressure on prices of the stimulus to expenditure compared with a stimulus to production.)

This also has implications in the open economy, especially if governments are fearful that a stimulus to economic activity in their own country will largely raise the demand for imports rather than domestic output. For the greater the extent to which the stimulus is provided initially by increasing the consumption of finished products, the greater the extent to which it is likely to result in a rise in imports, partly because its upward impact on prices will tend to make home production less competitive with imports, and partly because there is initially no additional output from domestic sources to set against this extra demand. (Indeed, the undue fears that exist in some countries – notably Britain – that there may be an excessive impact on imports if stimulatory measures are adopted presumably springs from past experience when the stimulus applied had usually been disproportionately in forms that stimulated *demand* rather than ones that stimulated *output* at the same time.)

By contrast, if the stimulus is primarily in forms that reduce the costs of production (reductions in payroll taxes or in employers' national insurance contributions, for example) the addition to employment that can be expected will be accompanied by (at least some) additional output, and the stimulus will therefore be in a form that tends to make domestic industry more competitive with imports, so that imports are likely to rise by less than they would have risen if the same stimulus to employment had been provided in the form of a stimulus to consumption demand.

This is not to imply that a country should always choose to give the stimulus initially to production rather than expenditure. But if it wants to prevent a large part of the rise in demand from being directed towards imports, this would be an argument for stimulating production rather than spending.

POLICY FOR A RESOURCE-RICH COUNTRY

When a country discovers and develops a resource – such as North Sea oil in Britain in the later 1970s, or a range of minerals in Australia in the early 1980s – it is important for it to adopt a combination of policy measures that does not make it harder for it to maintain a high level of employment, and to bring about the adaptation of its industrial structure in directions that will enable it to make the best possible use of its good fortune.

The risk is that the foreign exchange earnings associated with the additional exports may lead the country to adopt a combination of measures that will lead either to serious inflation or to serious unemployment (or both); and that it will fail to adopt a resource allocation policy (coupled with an appropriate macroeconomic policy) that will bring about the re-adjustment of the pattern of its output that is required if it is to put its good fortune to the best use.

One risk is that of inflation. If the country tries to prevent an appreciation, and merely allows the extra foreign exchange earnings to add to the country's reserves, without neutralising their effects on the country's liquidity, inflation will result, and imports will be sucked in largely as a result of the rise in prices. If the country in question fails to release enough resources from its least economic and most over-protected industries, this means that it will not be using the additional foreign exchange to purchase those items that it is most economic for it to import. For this reason, part of the appropriate adjustment ought certainly to be by way of ensuring that uneconomic import-competing industries are not maintained on an excessive scale as a result of protection or other forms of government assistance.

But it is not sufficient for the country to follow a resource allocation policy that releases resources from the less economic import-replacing industries. It is equally important to ensure that the real level of demand is kept high enough to ensure that the resources released from those industries are quickly re-employed elsewhere in the economy. The rise in overall productivity and potential living standards that results from the development of the mineral exports makes it important to maintain the real level of effective demand at an adequate level to absorb the extra output consequently becoming available to the economy; for otherwise it may in effect be used largely to provide benefits for those who become unemployed as a result of the failure to keep demand high enough to absorb the additional resources (and this is what appears to have happened to a large extent in Britain, and perhaps also in Australia, in 1979–81).

There is also a risk that an export boom may cause too high a level of demand if there is not also an adequate switch of demand towards imports. It is therefore important to combine a cut in tariffs, or in any quantitative restrictions that there may be on imports, or an appreciation, with an expansionary policy (preferably by way of tax cuts, so as to exert as much downward impact on prices as possible). Tariff cuts alone might well add to unemployment: the rise in exports alone might generate inflation. *Both* the expenditure-switching device of the tariff cuts *and* the appropriate expenditure-changing device of tax cuts are thus needed to ensure that the additional resources are put to good use without leading to either inflation or unemployment. The necessary increase in absorption at something close to full employment can sometimes occur in an inflationary manner (as in Australia in the Korean boom of 1950–1) by permitting a rise in prices with an under-valued exchange rate; but it is obviously best to cut tax rates and keep monetary policy tight enough to ensure that the exchange rate is kept strong and that the appropriate real stimulus to demand is provided with as little upward (or as much downward) effect as possible on the rate of inflation.

In short, the right prescription for such a situation is low taxes, tight monetary policy and low tariffs – a combination that seems often to be politically unattractive to most governments.

IS A MIX THAT HOLDS DOWN PRICES BY CAUSING AN APPRECIATION 'BEGGAR-MY-NEIGHBOUR'?

We have so far considered policy solely from the viewpoint of the country applying it. We shall now consider whether appropriate policies for combating stagflation are likely to have adverse effects on countries other than the one applying them.

If the choice of a mix that held down prices had an exactly symmetrical effect on the rest of the world (pushing up prices there), it would be reasonable to criticise it as being (to that extent) 'beggar-my-neighbour'. This might happen if the policy operated *solely* by causing an appreciation of the currency of the country concerned. But such criticism cannot logically be applied to most aspects of the arguments for using such a mix that have been advanced in this book.

The fundamental arguments for adopting relatively tight monetary policies coupled with low taxes, and for restraining those forms of government outlay that tend to raise prices at any given level of activity, do not depend upon appreciation for their operation, being valid for a closed economy (including the closed economy of the world) as well as for an open economy.

In the first place, so far as the choice of a mix with relatively tight monetary policy and low tax rates holds back inflation by improving productivity in the country applying the policy, this should also benefit the rest of the world, as it will tend to keep down the prices of that country's exports (at any given nominal exchange rate). Such a policy will thus certainly help the rest of the world to check inflation (provided, of course, that the rest of the world is not so misguided as to restrict imports from the country in question as a result of its exports having become more competitive in world markets).

Secondly, if the choice of mix helps to hold down money income demands and prices, but does not increase productivity at any given level of employment, the real exchange rate should not change, the nominal exchange rate moving in such a way as to offset the relatively slower rise in the price level of the country applying the policy. There will thus be no effect on the price level in other countries.

But, thirdly, it is true that so far as the choice of mix caused a net improvement of the capital account, the way in which this would check inflation in the country applying the policy would be to cause an appreciation of that country's currency that would have symmetrical (upward) effects on prices in the rest of the world. This effect (in contrast to the other effects outlined above) would be subsequently reversed, as higher interest and dividend payments to other countries resulted.

When the subsequent outflow of additional profits and dividends to other countries caused the exchange rate to move in the opposite direction, this would be helpful to countries in the rest of the world that were at that time trying to hold down inflation.

It is true that if all countries adopt the suggested mix simultaneously there is correspondingly less scope for any one of them to benefit by an appreciation resulting from capital inflow; but there will be correspondingly more scope for them all to benefit by having less inflation at any given level of employment so far as such a mix operates through the various 'closed economy' channels that have been described above.

In any case, so far as the mix under discussion operates through the capital account, and thus has symmetrical effects through the exchange rate on other countries not adopting a similar mix, it is not necessarily true that (even in the short run) those effects will cause as much deterioration in the macroeconomic situation of the rest of the world as the improvement that they bring about in the country applying the policy. For if the combination of tax cuts and tight monetary policy is applied mainly by those countries that are suffering from the worst stagflation the mix in question need not generate a corresponding worsening of stagflation in the rest of the world. For high tax rates coupled with an easy monetary policy may well have a greater relative effect in causing stagflation in countries where stagflation is already severe; and a given depreciation of the currency in a country that is *not* suffering from severe stagflation may well cause less upward pressure on the price level there than it would have done in a country where prices were already rising more rapidly. Moreover, if a country does not adopt a similar mix it is presumably because it is *not* suffering from such severe stagflation. If, on the other hand, its stagflation were no less severe than that of the country adopting this mix, then clearly such a mix would be equally appropriate to both countries.

But the main answer to the 'beggar-my-neighbour' argument is that if such a mix leads other countries to adopt a similar combination of measures, these policies will be mutually *reinforcing*; that is, they will help to solve the world's stagflationary problem – and will certainly not intensify it.

The term 'beggar-my-neighbour' as applied to certain types of remedies for unemployment was intended to characterise those policies during the 1930s that were intended to reduce unemployment by stimulating a country's exports and cutting its imports – such as competitive devaluations. But, as other countries retaliated, the stimulus to employment in the original country was negated, and the policies were therefore mutually *destructive* – in marked contrast to the use of devaluation to prevent adverse balance-of-payments effects resulting from simultaneously adopting stimulatory budgetary and monetary policies. (In this latter case, devaluation would not be 'beggar-my-neighbour', for it would simply have left the balance of payments unchanged by the combination of expansion and devaluation.)

In much the same way, an appreciation *that is accompanied by the adoption of a tight monetary policy mix by a country suffering from stagflation* could and should merely prevent the *depreciation* of its currency that would otherwise have occurred as a result of the expansionary measures themselves (which it had felt able to adopt only because they were accompanied by the switch of mix). A policy that combines an appropriate stimulus with the right sort of switch of mix should be good *both* for the country adopting it *and* for the world as a whole. It is true, however, on the other hand, that a country that tries to check inflation by policies that cause appreciation *alone* (without the stimulus) – as did Britain in 1979–80 – *whilst continuing to tolerate high and rising unemployment* deserves censure. But it deserves the censure for failing to cut taxes until the unemployment and the cost inflation disappear – *not* for keeping monetary policy tight (with consequent upward effects on the exchange rate). The appreciation would thus not occur if the overall setting of policy were expansionary enough. It would be absurd to criticise the proper use of a stimulatory policy by means of a mix involving tight monetary policy, simply as a result of confusing such a policy with the very different one of *deflation* coupled with high nominal interest rates such as practised in Britain in 1980. This sort of policy – a mix that causes appreciation *without* the stimulus to employment that a less inflationary mix makes possible – *is* appropriately described as 'beggar-my-neighbour'; for it worsens stagflation both in the country applying it and in the world as a whole.

Another possible line of criticism of a country that keeps its monetary policy tight is that the resulting flow of capital to it may force other countries to keep interest rates higher than they would otherwise have wished, and it is sometimes argued that this may reduce their ability to adopt expansionary measures. West Germany and Japan were said in late 1980 to be inhibited from adopting stimulatory monetary measures by fears of the capital outflow that would then result from interest rates being high in Britain and the USA. But a country with high tax rates (and those in West Germany were high by international standards in 1980) should in any event be trying to provide a stimulus by way of *tax cuts*; and any country that is concerned about inflation (as West Germany has always been) should in any event be trying to keep monetary policy tight and taxes low. If international pressure to do this (resulting from high interest rates elsewhere) increases the incentive for Germany to adopt a similar mix, then this pressure should be welcomed, rather than opposed. (It is true that in Japan the tax burden was not so high; but so long as there remains any risk of undue inflation a country cannot suffer macroeconomically from a mix that keeps monetary policy tight and taxes low.)

In short, it can only help to reduce the global problem of stagflation if as many countries as possible feel under pressure to adopt a mix of macroeconomic measures that will reduce their own stagflation – provided that this leads them to maintain a higher level of output and employment than they would have done if they had adopted a more inflationary mix.

CONCLUSION

For most countries, the serious external macroeconomic problems of the *past* were those of balance of payments deficits coupled with either excess demand or too much unemployment. When faced by the situation of *excess demand* combined with *external deficit* it is important that a country should use the least inflationary combination of measures – tight monetary policy coupled with cuts in those forms of government spending that tend to raise prices – to solve its internal and external problems. But the more topical problem of *external* deficit coupled with *stagflation* requires the use of a mix that includes tax cuts if the unemployment is to be reduced in the least inflationary way possible; for that will minimise any adverse effects of a stimulus on the balance of payments or on the exchange rate, especially if it is coupled with a sufficiently tight monetary policy.

When there is the special problem of *stagflation* coupled with a strong *balance of payments* – as in Britain in 1980/81 – it is understandable that businesses feel themselves weakened by the strong exchange rate. But the crucial question to ask in a period of stagflation is: what combination of measures will do most to reduce unemployment (and to stimulate industry) with the least upward (or greatest downward) effect on the price level? The answer to this question is *not* likely to be the politically popular one of easing monetary policy – partly to cause a depreciation; for that will cause more inflation for any given stimulus to industry than the same stimulus provided by way of tax cuts (or general subsidies). Taken alone, an easing of monetary policy would probably help the country's industries; but it would do so in a more inflationary way than would tax cuts. So long as the country is worried about cost-inflation, therefore, tax cuts are the appropriate remedy.[3]

In short, if a country is worried about inflation in any form, an easing of monetary policy, and consequent (temporary) depreciation, is to be avoided – yet it seems always to be politically attractive (and that is largely why world inflation rose to higher rates in recent decades). Where unemployment is too high, the net stimulus to be applied by way of tax cuts must be correspondingly greater; and when unemployment is low, monetary policy must be kept correspondingly tighter as taxes are cut to reduce cost inflation.

5 The Mix, the Budget and the National Debt

There are a number of aspects of policy relating to the budget that have a bearing on the proper use of the available macroeconomic policy instruments to stop stagflation. They include the question of how far the changes in the real level of the national debt may have implications for the appropriate combination of macroeconomic measures; and the relationship between the level of government spending that is thought appropriate for political or other reasons and the macroeconomic policy that should be followed. A more enlightened approach to these issues in general public discussion is essential if there is to be sufficient public understanding of the basic issues to ensure that the political obstacles to the adoption of appropriate policies are overcome.

IS THE 'BUDGET DEFICIT' IMPORTANT?

Excessive public attention has been devoted in recent years to the budget deficit (or surplus), or the Public Sector Borrowing Requirement (the 'PSBR') in Britain. Yet for a number of reasons the published figure for the outturn of the budget (the surplus or deficit) is not a good guide to the effect of the budget either on incomes or on the quantity of money. Nor does it give a reliable indication of whether the stance of budgetary policy is more expansionary than it would be if the deficit were lower. This is:

1. partly because the published figure for the actual outcome of the budget is not the best guide to the net effect of the budget;
2. partly because not only its net outturn, but also the absolute levels of government revenue and outlay are important; and
3. partly because the composition of each side of the budget (as between different types of outlays and different forms of revenue) are at least as important.

The following are some of the major limitations to the use of the net

The Mix, the Budget and the National Debt 69

budget outturn (the surplus or deficit) as an indication of the effects of budgetary policy, or of the direction in which budgetary policy should be changed.

1. In the first place, the actual surplus or deficit is the result of many factors in addition to the government's own policy decisions. When business activity is low, the deficit is relatively large because unemployment and other social-services payments as well as outlays on relief works, and deficits of nationalised industries, are high, whilst tax revenue is cyclically low. In this situation it is dangerously misleading to adopt the widespread practice of interpreting a relatively large budget deficit as an indication that policy is 'too expansionary'; for, so far as the deficit is high simply as a result of the recession, this ought, rather, to be taken as an indication that the setting of policy is not sufficiently expansionary. Attempts have been made to allow for this, by estimating what the budget deficit would be (with present policies) if a high level of employment prevailed. This is usually called the 'full employment' or 'high employment' budget deficit or surplus; but 'cyclically adjusted' deficit or surplus might be a better term for it. A more widespread use of such concepts, and a due allowance for them in all public statements and comments relating to the budget, would reduce the risk of governments feeling under pressure – as many of them did at times in the late 1970s and early 1980s – to make the budget even less expansionary than it was, simply because the recession had reduced revenue and increased certain types of outlays. Such policy reactions clearly depress activity (and revenue) still further. (One British minister aptly described such policies as 'The economics of the madhouse'.) If the reaction of the government is to raise tax rates, it also makes cost-inflation greater at any given level of activity.
2. There are many different levels of both government revenue and outlays that can produce the same figure for the budget deficit. The effect of the budget on incomes is related mainly to the absolute level of the budget, rather than to the net difference between the two sides of it.
3. The way in which a budget deficit is financed is also important in determining its effects. A given deficit may be consistent with a number of different changes in the quantity of money and in the financial structure of debt generally, according to whether it is financed by the creation of money or by borrowing from the non-bank public (and by what forms of debt), and according to its indirect effects upon banks and the balance of payments – the other main channels through which

70   *Unemployment, Inflation and New Macroeconomic Policy*

changes may occur in the quantity of money and in the financial structure.
4. Furthermore, so far as different forms of government outlay are known to have different effects on total demand, they should be distinguished from one another, and their consequences for total demand estimated accordingly. In particular, taxes and transfers have their effect on employment and output only after (and so far as) taxpayers or recipients change their spending as a consequence of the taxes or transfers; whereas incomes from productive activity are increased immediately (and to the full extent) when a government employs people to produce goods and services for it. Different sub-divisions of each of these outlays and revenues are also likely to have somewhat different effects; and, so far as they do so, it is still more misleading to try to assess the effects of a budget merely by looking at its net outturn or even at total outlays and total revenue.
5. If an entity that has previously been part of the public sector is sold off to private owners, but continues to undertake the same current and capital transactions with the public (and the government) the public sector deficit or surplus is likely to be affected but there is clearly no real change in the economy. Indeed, governments have even been known to advocate or undertake the sale to the public of shares in publicly owned enterprises *in order* to reduce the public sector deficit. This epitomises the absurdity of making a reduction in that deficit an aim of policy in itself.
6. Another respect in which the budget surplus or deficit is a misleading indication of the nature of the government's transactions is that it does not accurately measure the extent to which the government is borrowing (increasing the real value of the national debt) during the period in question. Part of the government's outgoings, in the form of interest on government debt, is in fact merely a compensation to owners of that debt for the fall in its real value as a result of inflation, and is thus a capital transaction. Moreover, there is nothing in the recorded budget figures to indicate the extent to which the real value of government debt outstanding is being reduced as a result of inflation, even though this constitutes a reduction in the government's indebtedness. The ordinary figures of the budget deficit are usually interpreted as an indication of the extent of the government's additional borrowing during the year in question, but they are a potentially very misleading guide to what has been happening to the real value of the national debt in a period of inflation. During the 1970s and early 1980s, the real level of the national debt in many countries had been rising much less than one would have

supposed by merely looking at the figures for nominal budget deficits, and in some countries it was falling in real terms in some of these years, even while nominal budget deficits were being recorded. A general public understanding of these considerations is necessary if obstacles that stand in the way of more rational budgetary policies are to be overcome. (These aspects are considered in more detail below, pp. 83–7.)

7. To all these considerations must be added the different relative effects on prices and employment of alternative budgetary measures discussed in Chapter 3.

For all these reasons it would be an aid to clearer thought about macroeconomic policy if attention were directed away from the net outturn of the budget and focused instead upon all the various constituents of the budget and on the way in which it is financed. We shall now consider certain ways in which undue preoccupation with certain narrowly budgetary objectives has made stagflation worse.

BUDGET DEFICITS AND RECESSION

If a government cuts its spending on goods and services, but leaves its budget balance *unchanged* (as a result of cutting taxes by an equal sum), there is likely to be a fall in national income and employment. But if at the same time it is trying to *reduce* the budget deficit – that is, to cut government spending by more than it is reducing its tax revenue – a fall in income and employment is more likely, and any fall is likely to be the greater. If it cuts the budget deficit by a given amount through tax increases, rather than by cuts in its spending, the consequent rise in cost-inflation will to that extent reduce the *real* quantity of money, and thus make total employment still more likely to fall – as well as raising prices. As the general effect of government policy over the period will thus be to hold down total income and employment, and to do so by tax increases (which are likely to cause particularly severe cuts in employment in the private sector), it is quite possible that the ratio of government spending to total output may actually rise – even though the government considers itself to be 'cutting' government spending. There is especially likely to be a rise in government outlays including transfers, as these tend to go up as a result of increases in unemployment during a recession. If the government feels committed to reducing the share of the public sector to total output this may well incline it to make further cuts in its own spending; and if it is also committed to trying to reduce the budget deficit its attempts to do this may be expected to increase unemployment still more – and so lead to the same vicious circle as before.

If a government is trying to reduce the share of government spending (as an aim in itself), and if, for unrelated reasons, there is then a recession, the restraint on government spending will make the recession worse than it need have been. Of course, this could be offset by a sufficiently large tax cut; but unless the government is willing to aim at increasing its budget deficit over the period (to a greater extent than if it had not curbed its outlays) the policy of trying to reduce the share of government spending to total output will further intensify the recession. (This seems to have happened, in Britain and Australia, for example, in the later years of the 1970s.)

The budget deficit and the share of the private sector in total output

Part of the political pressure in some countries to reduce the size of government borrowing appears to be motivated by the aim of reducing the size of the government sector in total output. But the two aims are by no means necessarily consistent; for a reduction in borrowing by the public sector is by no means a necessary or appropriate aim when a government is trying to reduce the relative size of the public sector. Whatever one's political preference about the relative size of the government and private sectors, therefore, they should not be confused with aims about the size of budget deficits.

The confusion of these two objectives with one another seems to have arisen because *one* way in which the budget deficit of a country may be reduced is, indeed, to reduce the level of government spending, whilst keeping taxation relatively constant. But it is equally possible to achieve the same reduction in the budget deficit by a *rise* in taxation on the private sector – and thus with a *reduction* in the size of the private sector. For the aim of reducing the budget deficit may lead the government in question to increase taxation by more than it reduces government spending; and the reduction in total income and output that results from the consequent overall setting of policy tends to maintain, or even increase, the relative size of the government sector in the economy, as a result of these attempts to reduce the budget deficit; for this mix of measures may be expected to affect the private sector (and total output) more adversely than it does the public sector.

In short, a government that tries simultaneously to reduce the budget deficit and to reduce the role of the government sector in a period of stagflation can expect to worsen either unemployment, or inflation, or both – and it may well not even succeed in reducing the ratio of government spending to total output, for such a policy may well reduce output more than it does government spending. If, therefore, the aim is to reduce the size of the government sector, it is likely to be necessary to *increase* the budget deficit if there is not to be a consequent rise in unemployment. Even a policy mix that involves reducing the ratio of government spending to total output does not necessarily mean that the actual level of government spending will ultimately be lower than it would otherwise have been. (With the other two mixes suggested above for stopping stagflation, government spending would be higher than otherwise.) For a cut in the *ratio* of government spending to total output coupled with a reduction in tax rates brings about a reduction in prices that the government would presumably have otherwise tried to achieve by operating the economy at a higher level of unemployment. In other words, if the alternative of a switch of mix is used (rather than a temporarily high level of unemployment), there will be a consequently higher level of output available, part of which can be utilised by the government. Especially if the loss of potential output that would have resulted from relying on deflation (rather than the switch of mix) would have been very large, it is quite possible, therefore, that the absolute level of government spending could actually have been higher if the deflationary policies were avoided and the switch of mix used instead. By the same token, a government that concentrates unduly on reducing government spending coupled with deflationary policies (lower levels of activity) will reduce its total outlays; but unless it also reduces tax rates to a sufficient extent (to offset the effects of the spending cuts on employment), total output and the real level of government spending will both be lower than if it had used an appropriate switch of policy mix instead of a reduction in output.

CAPITAL INVESTMENT AND THE BUDGET DEFICIT

Governments who believe that the budget deficit should be reduced – especially ones that start with the preconception that government spending is 'too high' in relation to total output – often resort to drastic cuts in government capital expenditures, which they usually find easier to cut than their current services to the public or the numbers or salaries of employees in the public sector. Yet costs of production may be increased in future as the result of cuts in certain types of expenditure on capital works (including capital expenditure on transportation), such as the provision of road or rail services; and such services are, in many cases, in the public sector. In Britain, for example, the fact that the railways are nationalised has led to considerable pressure on them to reduce their capital expenditure as a means of reducing the Public Sector Borrowing Requirement. Public investment in human capital, through education and training, is also often a prime

74 Unemployment, Inflation and New Macroeconomic Policy

target for cuts, as its adverse effects are mostly hard to measure, and they occur mainly in the distant future. The real economic, social and political costs of reducing a government's capital outlays become evident only in the longer run. Yet the size of the government's total outlays, and the amount that it can rationally try to borrow from the public, ought to be influenced by the extent to which outlays are for capital investment. In this sense, it is not defensible to cut capital outlays *in order* to reduce the budget deficit (or the PSBR in Britain). For the deficit at which the government should be aiming can reasonably be correspondingly higher if capital outlays are kept relatively high.

Similarly, a rise in the budget deficit that results from a cut in those forms of taxes that have been holding back private investment (or which results from a rise in subsidies to investment generally) may be justifiable even if the same deficit that was incurred for other purposes would not be justifiable. It is thus very dangerous to try to reduce the budget deficit to a particular figure without due attention to the effects of the cuts in outlays, or the rise in taxes, by means of which the deficit is being reduced. If a government does not succeed in achieving the restraint it had hoped for in its current outlays, it might do better to run a larger budget deficit than to try to balance its books by reducing desirable forms of capital outlay. (These are examples of the deficiencies of trying to use the budget deficit – or the PSBR – as a guide to policy or as an objective of policy; see the discussion on pp. 69–71.)

A PRICE-REDUCING STIMULUS THAT DOES NOT INCREASE THE DEFICIT

If a government wishes – perhaps for political reasons – to provide a price-reducing stimulus in a form that does not increase the budget deficit at a given level of unemployment, it is possible for it to do so, provided that it is paying some transfers in forms that are not holding down costs (or not as much as an equivalent tax cut would reduce them).

Even an equal cut in tax revenue and in *government spending on goods and services* might in some circumstances provide a price-reducing stimulus without a rise in the budget deficit. For some forms of tax cut might have such a large downward effect on the price level (together with those that might result from cutting some forms of government spending) that the resulting rise in the real quantity of money (and consequent reduction in real interest rates) might actually provide a stimulus to employment greater than the downward effect on job opportunities of the reduction in government spending on goods and services. But normally one would expect such a 'balanced budget contraction', *in this form*, to reduce employment.

It is, however, likely that an equal reduction in taxes and *transfer payments* would provide a price-reducing stimulus to activity. For an equal reduction in both tax revenue and transfer payments can normally be expected to have cost-reducing effects – whilst it will, of course, keep the budget surplus or deficit unchanged. The reduction in costs will occur because all taxes have some cost-increasing effects, whereas only those transfer payments by the government that hold down the general level of costs, or help to restrain wage increases, do so. Most subsidies to particular firms or industries are not likely to reduce costs generally, for if they assist less economic industries they reduce productivity; so that it is only those subsidies that are equally available to all industries that have general cost-reducing effects.

Most transfer payments, however, such as social security payments or subsidies to particular forms of outlay (housing or education, for instance) do not have any such general cost-reducing effects, or not to the same extent as a tax cut of the same size.

Moreover, an equal reduction in both taxes and transfers can be expected to have favourable effects on the incentive to work. The frequently heard claims that high tax rates have (net) disincentive effects cannot be accepted: for we do not know whether the adverse effect on incentives of the reduction in the reward for an extra hour of work will be fully (or more than fully) offset by the fact that the consequent reduction in income makes it more important to the taxpayer to earn extra income – and so to work harder. But an equal reduction in *both* tax payments *and* transfers must have net favourable effects upon incentives. For the total 'income' effect must be zero (apart from any distributional effects), as disposable income remains unchanged; whereas the favourable effect of the tax cuts on the incentive to work, rather than to take more leisure (the 'substitution' effect) will not be offset by a comparable effect through the cut in transfer payments, as these are not paid as a reward for work (and may even be paid as a reward for *not* working – as with unemployment benefits, pensions that are reduced when the pensioner takes paid employment, or payments to agricultural producers to keep land out of cultivation). So long as there remain any cost-increasing taxes and any transfer payments that are not holding down costs (as much as the taxes are increasing them), no government can reasonably argue that it is prevented from introducing a price-reducing stimulus merely because it is unwilling to increase the budget deficit.

Indeed, the budget deficit would fall as employment recovered if the price-reducing stimulus was given in this form of an equal cut in both transfers and taxes. By the same token, attempts to reduce the budget deficit in recent years may have been frustrated largely because increases in taxes and in transfer payments (together with price-increasing forms of government outlay) were so increasing the price level as to inflict higher unemployment on the economy as a result of the consequent reduction in the real quantity of money (with any given nominal quantity of money). The consequently higher unemployment then led to a rise in the deficit.

GOVERNMENT BORROWING AND THE QUANTITY OF MONEY

Governments often argue that if they have to borrow more, as a result of a rise in the budget deficit, this will tend to increase the quantity of money.

It is true as a definitional identity that a budget must be financed either by taxation, borrowing or the creation of money. But it is therefore not correct to state that a larger budget deficit must lead to the creation of more money. The expectation of governments that it will do so springs from their reluctance to offer the higher level of nominal interest rates that they expect to be necessary in order to finance a higher budget deficit by borrowing.

It is not certain, however, that a tax cut will lead, even temporarily, to higher nominal interest rates; for the resulting rise in nominal incomes will increase the demand for bonds as well as that for money; and before long the downward pressure on costs will help to reduce nominal interest rates. But so far as a rise in nominal interest rates may be the result, the reluctance of governments to cut taxes, if this increases the budget deficit, is a consequence of their having accepted some particular target for the level of nominal interest rates. In that case, then, any association there may be between a higher budget deficit and a faster rise in the quantity of money is a consequence of their adopting that pseudo-macroeconomic target, and not of the budget deficit as such.

INDEXATION OF INCOME-TAX RATES FOR INFLATION

Many countries have in recent years introduced some form of indexation of income-tax rates to allow for inflation. (They include Australia, Britain, Canada and Denmark – but not the USA, until 1984.) The purpose of adjusting nominal rates of income tax to allow for inflation is to make it necessary for governments to introduce new legislation if they wish to raise the *real* rates of tax (the proportion of a given real income taken in tax). Indexation prevents them from obtaining large increases in tax revenue in periods of rapid inflation (without passing legislation) merely as a result of the fact that income tax schedules are 'progressive' – meaning that as *nominal* incomes go up with inflation a rising proportion of them is payable in income tax.

One reason for the rapid expansion in government outlays during the first half of the 1970s was that the high rates of inflation produced windfall gains in tax revenue, so that unpopular legislation to raise taxation was not necessary in order to finance the increased outlays. Governments usually try to resist any automatic indexation of income-tax rates, unless their party has committed itself to it when in opposition. One reason is that it deprives them of the possibility of claiming that they have 'cut' tax rates, when they have merely avoided, or alleviated, the rise in real rates that would otherwise have resulted from inflation.

Various objections (of little or no validity) have been made to automatic indexation. One such objection is the argument that no *automatic* adjustment of rates can be what is best for the country, and the government therefore ought to be continually revising the tax structure as may be necessary. But the proposal for automatic indexation is – or should be – merely that *legislation has to be introduced* in order to raise real tax rates. The provision for automatic indexation should merely ensure that real tax rates do not rise fortuitously, haphazardly and accidentally, as a result of inflation; to *ensure* in fact that real tax rates *are* revised according to need every year. It would be more to the point to argue that *without* indexation the level of real tax rates is likely to rise unpredictably and excessively – or at least to an extent that is not consciously tailored to the economic requirements of the country. But a government can and must always consider whether the real rates remaining after automatic indexation are those best suited to the current situation.

A practical difficulty that has been raised in some quarters is the problem of what index to use to adjust nominal rates. But *any* reasonable index of inflation will be better than none. It is, however, important that governments should not be free to adjust the index themselves – as has occurred in Australia – for example to allow for what they claim to be their estimate of the upward effect on the index of indirect-tax increases that they have themselves introduced. For that enables them to introduce increases in real income-tax rates by stealth (so to speak) – merely as a by-product of a rise in indirect taxes, if that has (or if the government claims that it has) upward effects on the price level. For if nominal income-tax rates are not adjusted downwards for those rises in prices that are claimed to be the consequence of increases in indirect tax rates, this means that increases in the latter will, in effect, result in increases in real income-tax rates as well – without any legislation to that effect.

In the context of the present book, the importance of the automatic indexation of income-tax rates is that it makes it less likely that governments will allow taxation (and government spending) to rise to excessively high levels. The period when cost-push inflation arising from increased levels of taxation in relation to total output was at its worst in most countries was that of rapid inflation during the years 1973–5, before it had become the practice for many countries to introduce automatic indexation. (In the US the issue became important only with the high rates of inflation in the later 1970s.)

A further misplaced objection that some may raise to adjusting nominal income-tax rates for inflation is that taxable income may not rise when prices rise. For example, imported inflation (perhaps resulting from increased prices of imported oil) may raise the price level when domestic money incomes are not rising fully in proportion to the price level. But even if domestic money incomes are constant, the rise in the price of imports purchased out of those incomes means that real incomes have fallen – so that unchanged nominal tax rates would have amounted to a rise in real tax rates. It is just as important to adjust nominal income-tax rates downwards when the fall in real incomes is due to higher prices paid by the income-earners as when it is associated with increases in their money incomes. So far as the higher cost of imports necessitates a reduction in the country's real post-tax incomes, this should be achieved by whatever is the most efficient combination of measures – and not as an accidental result of an unlegislated rise in effective income-tax rates.[1]

THE POLICY MIX AND THE NATIONAL DEBT

Although some people may hope that cuts in tax rates could actually raise total tax revenue in some circumstances, one must assume that any mix involving tax cuts (except one that simultaneously reduces certain transfer payments by the same amount) will lead to a rise in the government's borrowing requirement *at any given level of employment*.

The adoption of such cost-reducing mixes would, however, presumably make it unnecessary to tolerate as high a level of unemployment as would otherwise have been permitted (in the hope that it would reduce inflation over the period in question). If so, the consequently higher level of employment and output that would become possible with the adoption of the proposed mixes would tend to increase tax revenue, and would reduce outlays on unemployment benefits and on some other forms of social-services payments, as well as reducing outlays for the support of nationalised industries and on relief works for the unemployed. But so far as government borrowing does rise as a result of adopting one of the suggested mixes, it is reasonable to ask whether this would make it necessary for posterity to levy taxes that would have cost-increasing effects comparable to those that we would be avoiding in the near future by cutting tax rates now: and, if so, whether this consideration ought to inhibit us from using such policy mixes to stop stagflation now.[2]

In any discussions of the relevance of the level of the national debt, widespread popular fallacies are liable to cloud the issue. It is as well, therefore, to make it clear at the outset that the present generation can use only the goods and services being produced now; just as future generations can use only the goods and services being produced by them. There is no possibility of one generation somehow using a higher level of government borrowing to transfer goods and services from one point of time to another. (One generation can, however, in other ways alter the amount of exhaustible resources, or the stock of human and material capital, that it bequeaths to posterity, by many of its policy decisions.) The level of government borrowing that occurs today may well, however, affect the *allocation* of resources and the *distribution* of income in future years.

The other widespread misconception that requires to be corrected is that government borrowing is somehow inherently different from that undertaken by the private sector. A given loan for financing a particular capital project must be assumed to have the same effect, whether it is the government or a private business that undertakes the project. If there are differences in the effects they can only be because the government puts the resources to a different use from that to which they would have been applied in the private sector. But the ensuing analysis is largely concerned, not with government borrowing to finance its own capital projects, but with borrowing by the government in order to make possible lower tax rates, and therefore to make possible in this way a higher level of private spending.

Nor should the repayment of principal and the payment of interest on a public loan have inherently different characteristics from the same process when similar payments are being made on a private loan. Governments may impose taxes in order to service the loan (or, more exactly, to hold down total spending to what the country can afford in the light of the interest payments being made to its debtors). These taxes may well be expected to raise the prices of the goods on which they are imposed (which could well be the products of the project financed by the loan). In the same way, the private sector may pay interest out of the revenue it receives from charging appropriately higher prices on the goods produced by the project.

Most analyses of questions relating to the national debt are made on the assumption of a given level of activity (now and also in the future). The present analysis, however, is concerned with using a higher level of government borrowing coupled with tax cuts, to avoid tolerating unemployment as an alternative measure for attempting to check inflation in the present and immediate future. The benefit to the country of the government borrowing in question is, therefore, primarily the higher output that becomes possible as a result of this tax cut and bond sale. During the 1970s, when governments were often borrowing at a low, zero or even negative real post-tax rate of interest, clearly there was certain to be a net social benefit to be derived from any bond sale (to make possible a tax cut) that enabled a higher level of employment and output to occur.

Effect on future real incomes

If we use a switch of mix to check inflation instead of tolerating temporarily higher unemployment, some of the extra output that results from the consequently fuller use of our economic potential (including productivity increases at each level of employment) will presumably be used to bequeath to posterity a higher stock of physical and human capital. Not only will some of the extra output presumably be devoted to producing capital goods (which will yield some of their return in future), but the consequently higher level of employment in the present will make it possible to avoid the lamentable waste of potential human capital that results when people who are unemployed are consequently unable to develop the skills and work habits that enable them to be fully productive members of the work force. Such a policy giving these people employment would increase their potential future contribution to the country's economic welfare, and this will enable posterity to meet at least some of the extra demands that may be exercised by those who receive the extra interest on the national debt resulting from the larger sales of government securities to the public in earlier years. Indeed, this higher level of goods and services could even exceed the extra consumption by the earners of the interest – especially if they were in income groups that saved a high proportion of this addition to their income, or if the overcoming of stagflation led to a rise in the proportion of their income that people saved. It should also be borne in mind that one effect in the shorter run of raising nominal interest rates would be a lower level of spending by the owners of existing debt; though that effect would be reversed subsequently, as lower inflation led to lower nominal interest rates.

Furthermore, any rise in interest payments on government debt would not constitute a corresponding net rise in the interest income of the recipients; for they would presumably be lending less to private industry (at any given level of real income) as the lower rates of taxation would have reduced the need of private industry to borrow in the period when the extra government debt was being issued. But so far as government interest payments raised the level of (post-tax) income, some measure would presumably have to be introduced to offset the upward effect on demand of any consequent rise in consumption by the recipients of the interest – if this were not fully offset by the higher level of output made possible for posterity by the consequently greater success in stopping stagflation. These measures might be cuts in some form of government spending (or a tighter monetary policy) – which might inflict some welfare cost, but would presumably not make inflation worse. But let us consider the consequences of imposing a higher level of tax (than would otherwise have been chosen) in future, if that were made necessary by the higher level of interest payments being earned on government bonds.

Effects on future inflation

We have seen that the higher productivity levels in future that can be expected if we stop stagflation will make it easier to hold down prices in future. On the other hand, we have seen that, at any given level of activity, there may be a consequent rise in net interest receipts in future, which may give rise to some extra consumption that would need to be held down by the imposition of some additional taxation. Would any such additional taxes present so serious a problem for posterity that it ought to inhibit us from cutting taxes and selling bonds to the public now? We would clearly need a very strong presumption that this would be so before we should allow that consideration to persuade us to tolerate high unemployment now rather than to cut taxes (while selling sufficient by way of attractive government bonds) to enable us to restore full employment without inflation. But there is certainly no presumption that any such self-denial on our part would be in the long-run social interest.

In the first place, if we stop stagflation our example may well help posterity to do the same; and if we suffer less upward pressure on the price level as a result of adopting a more appropriate mix, the fact that people will have experienced less inflation in the near future will help to hold down the expected, and so the actual, rate of inflation in the more distant future; and that will help to solve the problem of inflation into the indefinite future.

In any case, we have no reason to assume that the main macroeconomic problem of posterity will be the same as ours. (For all we know, the problem of the 1990s might even be excessively *falling* prices.) In any case the cost-inflationary effects of high taxes would not be such a worry in future decades unless stagflation proves to be as great a problem for them as for us.

But even if the macroeconomic problems of posterity turn out to be the same as ours, there is no reason to assume that tax cuts (coupled with bond sales) at the present time mean that we shall be imposing the same degree of tax-push inflation on them. For one thing, there is no presumption that a given cut in our present tax rates, accompanied by higher government borrowing, will necessitate an equal rise in tax rates in future. But even if it meant that posterity had to suffer a *rise* in tax rates comparable to the *cut* we were making in ours, it might be starting from a lower general level of tax rates than ours. With a larger output than ours, even the same level of revenue could in future be raised with lower tax rates. Furthermore, even the same general level of tax rates might be expected to have less cost-push effect if real living standards are higher in future; for that might well make future generations less dissatisfied with any given pre-tax wage increase, and so less likely to bid up their money incomes or to divert effort to avoiding and evading taxes.

Moreover, even if tax cuts now meant more or less comparable tax increases for posterity, and if this caused them as much dissatisfaction as higher tax rates would cause us, we may reasonably decide to discount this cost to posterity if they are expected to be wealthier than we are; and the extent to which they are likely to be wealthier than we are will be increased if we overcome stagflation quickly, and consequently bequeath to posterity a larger stock of human and material capital. It is customary, in any case, to discount the costs we may be imposing on posterity at some appreciable rate; and so far as we continue to do this in our policy decisions it would incline us to concentrate on solving our own problems and leaving posterity to look after itself. As, in this case, there is a clear expectation that success in stopping stagflation now will bring benefit to posterity as a result of the larger capital stock and higher productivity that will result, there is no good reason to refrain from tax cuts and bond sales now merely in the fear that we might be thereby inflicting some other cost on posterity; for, as we have seen, there is no convincing balance of argument to suggest that any rise in tax rates that would consequently have to be imposed by posterity would present future generations with greater macroeconomic problems than we would be avoiding by cutting taxes and selling the extra bonds.

In any case, these considerations have to be set against the more general question of whether the national debt is (for other reasons) rising rapidly in relation to income.

The level of the national debt

The case for cutting taxes and selling bonds, instead of tolerating high

The Mix, the Budget and the National Debt 83

unemployment as a policy for trying to check inflation, is valid in principle whatever changes may be occurring in the national debt for other reasons. Yet some people would be more inclined to adopt a mix that involves a rise in the nominal level of the national debt if the actual debt were falling (or not rising rapidly) in relation to the national income; and so far as that would be one consideration affecting the tax rates that posterity might have to levy, there would be some rationale for adopting that approach.

But, in any case, before one could argue that the national debt should or should not be allowed to rise more rapidly one ought to take account of the reasons why any current rise in the national debt is occurring. There are various valid arguments for a government to borrow. In particular, if it borrows to finance a capital project the relevant arguments are exactly the same as they are for a privately financed capital project; in either case the repayment of principal and the interest payments may be financed out of the additional output made possible by the project. If a government borrows to make possible a tax cut which enables a firm to finance a capital project, clearly, in effect, the government is acting more or less as an intermediary between borrower and lender; the real situation is virtually the same as if the firm were borrowing the finance itself, especially if the government subsequently taxes the firm to pay the interest and repay the debt.

Moreover, in a period of recession, even those who advocate that governments should balance their budgets over good and bad years together would agree that deficits incurred for cyclical purposes are defensible. It is therefore remarkable that in many countries in the later 1970s, many governments (even ones undertaking considerable capital investment) were not in fact raising the national debt in real terms, at least after allowance for cyclical factors, in proportion to national income. For Britain and the USA during the 1970s there was certainly not a clear upward trend in the relation of national debt in market hands to GDP, at least after due allowance for the fact that the later years were marked by the deepest post-war recession.[3] These facts are at least consistent with the view that governments were probably borrowing too little to maintain full employment – even though their preference for creating debt in monetary forms (rather than by selling bonds yielding a positive real post-tax return) was tending to raise the price level at any given level of employment.

Real changes in the national debt

Public attention is usually focused exclusively on the nominal budget deficit (or 'borrowing requirement') for the current year, whereas the equally (or more) important changes in the national debt that result from price changes receive very little publicity. This fact has played an important role in perpetuating macroeconomic policies that have caused stagflation. For governments have in recent years often felt under pressure from public opinion to reduce their net borrowing in nominal terms – even when the real level of their net borrowing was much smaller than the nominal figure, and when in some years it was even negative (a net reduction in the real value of the national debt). Failure to view these matters in real terms thus presumably led to more deflationary policies than would have otherwise been adopted. It may facilitate understanding of these matters if a very simple arithmetical illustrative example is given.

Let us consider first a situation where the budget is balanced – current revenue exactly equalling current expenditure of all types, so that in nominal terms the government is neither issuing new debt nor repaying old debt. But suppose that there is in existence 1000 million (in national currency units) of bonds held by the non-bank public. In a year in which prices rise by 10 per cent the real value of these bonds to their holders has fallen by 10 per cent, just as surely as it would have done if prices had been stable and the government had unilaterally written the debt down by 100 million currency units. This constitutes dissaving by the holders of the bonds; for to that extent they have been failing to live within their income to a sufficient extent to maintain the real value of their financial assets – whilst the government (on behalf of the taxpayer) will have reduced its outstanding obligations by 10 per cent in real terms – which is in that sense equivalent to a net repayment or, rather, a (unilateral) cancellation of debt. (This form of dissaving by the public – and saving by the government – is not included in the normal statistical measurements of net national saving.)

Now let us consider the situation where there is no outstanding debt, but the government runs a deficit of 100 units. If prices are stable this means that a national debt of 100 units has been created, but if prices were rising by 10 per cent these would be worth only 90 units, in terms of the prices prevailing at the beginning of the year.

Let us now put together these two changes – a rise in the price level of 10 per cent when there is an outstanding debt of 1000 units and a budget deficit of 100 units in the current year. So far as the real value of the national debt depends on the effect of inflation on the existing debt, it has fallen during the year by 100 (in terms of the prices prevailing at the beginning of the year); whilst it has risen by 90 of those units as a result of the current budget deficit (when adjusted for inflation). In net terms, therefore, the real value of the debt has fallen by 10 units in terms of the prices prevailing at the beginning of the year, or by 1 per cent in real terms.

During the 1970s the effect of inflation in reducing the real value of the national debt outstanding offset much of the addition to the debt as bonds were sold to the public to finance the nominal budget deficits of those years. Whatever the arguments for increasing or reducing the real value of the national debt outstanding, most people would feel it more appropriate to run budget deficits (and less justifiable to run budget surpluses) in a country where the national debt is not rising markedly in relation to output (after allowing for cyclical factors). Unfortunately, the constant reference in popular discussion to *nominal* budget deficits (or the 'PSBR') as a measure of government borrowing (and the lack of any comparable degree of publicity for estimates of the *real* change in the national debt) led to the widespread impression that budgetary policies had been very 'expansionary' – whereas in fact the real net level of government borrowing had been much lower than the level of the nominal budget deficits made it appear; and had in some countries even been negative, especially if the budget is adjusted for cyclical factors. This meant that in the second half of the 1970s and in the early 1980s government budgetary policies were generally very deflationary.

This situation is consistent with the view that governments were borrowing too little and taxing too much (though it does not of course *prove* that assertion). At the very least, the real change in the (interest-bearing) national debt in most countries in the 1970s was not such as to constitute a persuasive argument *against* adopting a policy that would raise less by way of taxation and more by borrowing from the non-bank public; even though the rise in the *non-interest bearing debt* (the quantity of money) *was* excessive, in that the manner in which it was created tended to raise the price level at any given level of employment.

The real national debt and deflationary policies

The widespread belief that the rise in the real level of the national debt – the real deficit – was greater than it was in fact during the later 1970s clearly led governments to adopt less expansionary policies than they would otherwise have done. The reduction in the real value of people's holdings of government bonds (as a result of inflation) led them (subsequently) to increase their saving (as normally measured); whilst the emphasis on the *nominal* budget deficit in public discussion and official statements led to the adoption of even less expansionary budgetary policies, whereas *more* expansionary ones would have been necessary if budgetary policies were to have offset the deflationary effect of the higher rate of saving by the public.

On the one hand, therefore, the fall in the real value of the stock of government securities outstanding, as a consequence of the rise in the price level, indirectly made unemployment worse in later periods by encouraging additional saving; whilst, on the other hand, the government's emphasis on the nominal budget deficit (and lack of due attention to the other influences on the real level of the national debt) led governments to adopt budgetary policies that made unemployment worse. It would have been more logical for governments to react to the fall in the real value of the outstanding debt (through inflation) by saving *less*.

Moreover, it was not merely that the combined effect of these two factors led to higher unemployment than would otherwise have prevailed; it often led them to adopt a mix of measures that made inflation worse at that level of unemployment. For the reluctance of governments to run the risk of a large (nominal) budget deficit meant that if they took steps to hold down unemployment they were more inclined to do so by the relatively inflationary means of an easing of monetary policy, as they wished to avoid the rise in the budget deficit that would have resulted from tax cuts. It is thus ironic that governments who defended their opposition to larger budget deficits on the grounds that they feared that such a policy would lead to a faster growth of the quantity of money, were consequently forced to adopt a mix with a more expansionary monetary policy, with a faster rise in the quantity of money than would have been necessary if budgetary policy had been more expansionary. By contrast, a due recognition of the lower *real* level of the outstanding stock of government securities (at least in relation to the trend value of total output) that resulted from inflation, would have led to more attention being given to the need to provide adequate amounts of reasonably attractive (or, at least 'honest') securities for the public, and greater readiness to run (appropriately financed) budget deficits, and so to a greater willingness to cut tax rates.

The upshot was, then, that the measures employed – easier monetary policies than were really appropriate, plus higher taxes than were desirable – exerted further upward pressure on prices, causing further reductions in the real value of the outstanding stock of government securities, and a further consequent twist of the stagflationary spiral.

One would hope that many economic advisers (if not the responsible ministers themselves) were well aware of this state of affairs. But (if so) presumably they did not emphasise it: indeed, they probably kept quiet about it in most countries and for most of the time, largely because they feared the proclivity of politicians to run irresponsibly large deficits financed in inappropriate ways, if the politicians had been provided in this way with an apparent excuse for doing so. If, however, the distinction had been firmly drawn between financing deficits by the creation of money (on the one hand) and financing them by creating adequate amounts of interest-bearing financial assets of types that the public was willing to hold (on the other), excessive cash deficits could have been avoided. The difficulty faced by economic advisers (to view the matter as charitably as possible) was presumably that they usually felt that they had to operate within the constraint that politicians would not accept the rise in nominal interest rates that they expected would be the result (in the short run at least) of cutting taxes and selling bonds on an adequate scale.

But economists generally ought to share part of the blame for failing to emphasise adequately the difference between nominal and real changes in the national debt, and the need to distinguish deficits financed by the creation of money from deficits financed in less inflationary ways. The whole approach to macroeconomic analysis in the past failed to distinguish the different effects on the price level of alternative types of stimulatory policies. This deficiency thus left the way open to people to oppose responsible, non-inflationary forms of stimulus, simply by failing to distinguish these from the use of inflationary policies that provide the stimulus by easy monetary policies and deficits financed by the creation of money. The political opposition in many countries must likewise bear a very large share of the blame for so often urging governments to try to hold down nominal interest rates (by expansionary monetary measures).

CONCLUSION ON THE MIX AND THE NATIONAL DEBT

For a country suffering from stagflation, a tax cut coupled with an appropriate sale of bonds to the public is likely to reduce inflation (at any given level of employment) in the near future and so to make the government feel able to operate the economy at a higher level of activity. This will benefit posterity as well as the present generation, and will justify a higher net level of government borrowing than would otherwise have been appropriate. Even if this means that posterity will have to impose higher tax rates than would otherwise have been necessary, the consequent rise in the tax rates paid by posterity will not necessarily be as great as the reduction in tax rates now; and in so far as the taxes paid by posterity do consequently rise, this may not cause posterity as much cost inflation as the same taxes imposed now. Moreover, if their real living standards are higher than ours, they will be better able to withstand the same (or even higher) taxes without suffering as much cost inflation as we are suffering (from any given tax rate); and if we *fail* to stop stagflation it will become less likely that their living standards will be higher than ours. In any case, the national debt and the interest on it may in future be at a lower ratio to total output than they are now, and taxes may also be lower for other reasons. If so, the same rise in tax payments will represent less of a burden (in all the relevant senses) for posterity than it would for us. Posterity may also be less worried about cost inflation than we are.

In any case, the favourable productivity effects of a mix with lower tax rates (now), and the consequently higher level of output and investment in the near future, will enable posterity to produce (with its consequently larger stock of capital) more goods and services to be purchased by the recipients of the extra interest.

It must also be stressed that if we are successful in adopting a mix that holds down the rate of inflation in the immediate future, that success will have some effect in reducing the rate of inflation that is expected by posterity, because they will have consequently experienced lower rates of inflation (in preceding years). Even the same rates of tax as ours might thus have less effect in raising the actual and expected rate of inflation in future, as a result of being imposed in a period when people will have been experiencing in the recent past lower rates of inflation than we have been experiencing during the past decade or so.

Indeed, we do not know what combination of macroeconomic problems will be the main concern of posterity. During the 1930s people would not have foreseen that the main problem of the next few decades was to be the prevention of inflation rather than unemployment; and during the 1950s and 1960s one could not have foreseen that the problem of the 1970s and early 1980s (at least) was to be the combination of both unemployment and inflation. It is true that if the problem of posterity continues to be inflation at less than full employment it will be a disadvantage to posterity to have high tax rates. But if inflation coupled with high unemployment does not turn out to be the main macroeconomic problem for posterity, then it would obviously have been correspondingly less rational for us to refrain from cutting taxes now merely because of fears that such a policy might involve posterity in levying higher taxes than would otherwise have been necessary.

If a case was to be made out for tolerating temporarily high unemployment in the hope that it would check inflation, rather than using a mix that involved tax cuts and bond sales, it would be necessary to argue that the latter policy would inflict at least as much social cost by way of extra inflation, unemployment, or other costs on posterity as it would bring social benefit to us; and that we ought to give so much weight to this consideration in formulating our own policies as to preclude the use of the policy mix in question. The arguments outlined above suggest, however, that there is no prima facie case for the view that posterity would be more likely to suffer if we *failed* to use a more appropriate mix to stop stagflation. It would certainly

The Mix, the Budget and the National Debt 89

be indefensible to inflict on the present generation the social and economic costs of high unemployment without explicitly considering these issues and convincingly demonstrating that a policy of tax cuts and bond sales now would inflict disproportionate costs on posterity. Yet, so far from any such case having been argued in defence of the deflationary policies adopted in recent years, it seems never to have been even addressed in any public defence of the policies in question. Starting from the position that prevails in most OECD countries at the beginning of the 1980s, the most useful guiding principle to adopt is that the best thing we can do for posterity is to stop stagflation; and that lower tax rates and a higher level of government borrowing (at attractive real post-tax interest rates to the lender) are likely to be important elements in such a policy. But if that policy were thought likely to inflict disproportionate costs on posterity, the mix involving equal reductions in tax revenue and transfer payments (which clearly does not increase government borrowing) would then be correspondingly more appropriate.

6 Resource Allocation Policy and Macroeconomic Policy

The various policy measures by means of which governments affect the allocation of resources – including tariffs, taxes and subsidies on particular forms of production and consumption, direct controls (including import controls) and their own purchasing policy – interact with macroeconomic policy in both directions.

On the one hand, resource allocation policies themselves have important effects on the price level by affecting the productivity of the economy. For assistance to relatively uneconomic industries means that a country is obtaining a lower real output than it might from the resources that it is using. For any given money income, or any given level of employment, this means that the price level will be higher than it would have been with a better allocation of resources. Measures that improve the allocation of resources reduce price increases over the period in which they are taking place, and ones that worsen it make it harder to control inflation over the period in question. Governments can affect only employment *in particular industries* by measures that give assistance to those industries; there is no reason to believe that they can do anything to increase *total* employment in the economy by such differential measures. Good macroeconomic management can ensure full employment at any given setting of tariff and other barriers to trade. But governments that wish to hold down prices (at any given level of employment) would be well advised to reduce or remove the many barriers to trade and to an economic allocation of resources.

Yet many uneconomic industries ask for, and often receive, special forms of assistance to protect them from unemployment in recessions; and the differential assistance given to those industries tends to reduce output per head (in real terms), and so raise prices. The increase in prices associated with the granting of additional protection is rapidly felt in the less sheltered sectors of the economy in the form of a cost-price squeeze, especially in an environment where price increases feed quickly through into increases in money wage rates and general cost levels. Export industries, in particular, are poorly placed to pass on increases in their domestic costs to overseas customers who buy on world markets. Stagflation consequently becomes worse in the country applying the policies.

On the other hand, macroeconomic policies also affect resource allocation policies. When (for whatever reasons) those responsible for macroeconomic management fail to maintain a high level of employment, the political pressures for increases in various forms of protectionism increase – for tariffs or import controls against imports competing with certain domestic industries, or for tax cuts or subsidies to favour particular forms of production. It is particularly difficult in times of recession for governments to resist political calls for protection, as was shown in the 1930s, and as has also been shown (though on a smaller scale) in the situation of stagflation in the later 1970s and early 1980s.

Furthermore, there is a vicious circle between these two sorts of interactions. For when unemployment is high, and certain weak industries call for greater governmental assistance, as they are usually among the less economic industries the consequent rise in the price level tends to make governments tolerate higher general levels of unemployment, in the hope of checking the consequent upward pressure on prices. The cycle then begins again, with additional demands for assistance from the industries that now find themselves most threatened as a result of the deflationary policies that the government has adopted in the hope of reducing inflation.

In the same way, policies that support monopolies and restrictive practices or (as in the EEC) promote the formation of cartels during recessions, tend to raise the price level generally by worsening the allocation of resources, and so make it harder to hold down inflation. Again, if governments react by trying to check inflation by tolerating longer periods of high unemployment, the problem of stagflation is worsened, and another vicious circle is likely.

RESOURCE ALLOCATION POLICY AND STAGFLATION

Whenever a government is tolerating a temporarily higher level of unemployment than it would otherwise have done, in the hope of thereby exerting some downward effect on the rate of inflation over a certain period, it is illogical for it simultaneously to protect less economic industries with the aim of keeping down the unemployment. For not only does this tend to raise the price level, but if the government really believes that unemployment is an effective cure for inflation, and if it believes there is no other cure available, presumably it ought to want to keep unemployment *up*, rather than to reduce it. If it wants to smooth the re-allocation of employment to other industries, additional protection for the declining industries will not encourage such structural adjustment; it would be better to assist people in those industries to re-train and to re-settle in areas where the new jobs are to become available.

But the main reason why such a policy is irrational in a period of stagflation is that the upward effect on prices that results from protecting the less economic industries makes it harder to bring down the rate of inflation in any given period and with any given level of unemployment. In other words, it makes it necessary to tolerate more unemployment, over the relevant period, than would otherwise have been required in order to bring down inflation by a given amount (if that would in fact be an effective way of reducing inflation).

These arguments for a resource-allocation policy attuned to the needs of a stagflationary situation – which means the exact opposite of the sort of policy that most western economies have been applying – is independent of the arguments outlined in earlier chapters for adopting a better mix of macroeconomic instruments for stopping stagflation. For the point about the relevance of resource-allocation policy would be just as valid even if all the available macroeconomic instruments had exactly the same effect on the price level for any given effect on employment. The only real connection between the two groups of policy issues is that if governments were continually asking themselves the important basic question – 'What combination of measures will do most to minimise the upward pressure on prices at any given level of unemployment?' – they would be unlikely (for example) to apply resource-allocation policies that hold down low-cost imports of foodstuffs and textiles, particularly as those categories of products figure prominently in the most widely used indexes of retail prices. An approach that was continually considering the relative effects of different measures (including import controls, tariffs and so on) on prices and employment could not logically lead to the adoption of policies to protect uneconomic industries; for such policies exert upward pressure on prices at any given level of unemployment.

An increase in assistance to less economic industries (or to less economic firms or mines) is not a reversal of policy (a 'U-turn'); it is, rather, 'more of the same'. For the policy of giving assistance to relatively 'lame-duck' industries, whilst keeping the *general* level of activity low, is a combination of measures likely to *increase* the amount of unemployment needed to achieve a given reduction in inflation; and further assistance to uneconomic industries (or firms, or mines) merely continues the wrong allocation of policy instruments. For resource-allocation policy instruments – such as tariffs and quotas, and subsidies to particular industries – are not suitable measures for macroeconomic management. They can be used to keep down sectional, or regional, but not *aggregate* unemployment: jobs saved in textiles destroy jobs in exporting industries and in the domestic industries that would have supplied the exporting industries. Only general measures of macroeconomic policy can reduce general unemployment. At the same time, whenever additional protection is given an industry, this is likely to cause cost and price increases that lead governments to tolerate high general unemployment.

In short, the two groups of economic problems and policies need to be tackled in an integrated way; but each involves the use of different groups of instruments if it is to be handled properly. A sound resource-allocation policy is unlikely to be adopted so long as governments try to tackle stagflation by tolerating high unemployment; whilst defective resource-allocation policies make it harder to stop stagflation.

Can unemployment be 'good for growth'?

Governments that are resorting to policies that involve the use of unemployment in the hope of thereby checking inflation often argue that in the long run this will be 'good for growth', as the reduction in the rate of inflation is a precondition for achieving a higher rate of growth.

This argument depends on four basic assumptions, none of which is likely to be valid.

1. It assumes that inflation in itself is the main obstacle to investment and growth, whereas stagflation – the combination of both unemployment and inflation – is in fact a still greater obstacle to a high level of productive investment. Indeed, the element of high unemployment in stagflation is likely to be more unfavourable to business confidence than is the element of inflation (which in some circumstances might even encourage productive investment).
2. It assumes that high unemployment will stop inflation, whereas this may not be true, especially when output has already been reduced well below capacity, and if the mix of measures used to hold up unemployment is itself a price-increasing one (with high tax rates, high government spending in forms that are likely to hold up prices, and low or negative real post-tax interest rates).
3. It assumes that there is no way of reducing the rate of inflation over the period in question apart from policies that keep unemployment at a temporarily high level; whereas a switch of mix in an anti-inflationary direction could have this effect without the need to create the unemployment.

4. It assumes that the policy of tolerating temporarily high unemployment will have such a great upward effect on real output in the long run as to more than offset the loss of output associated with the high unemployment in the short run. But even if the unemployment did reduce inflation (and if there were no other way of doing this) it is unlikely that any consequent future rise in output would be sufficient to equal or offset the loss of output associated with the high unemployment in the immediate future – at least on the scale of the later 1970s and early 1980s.

Can recessions increase productivity?

Some proponents of deflationary policies – in Britain, especially – have argued that recession can produce a 'shake-out' which will lead to a 'structural adjustment' of a country's industry in desirable directions.

It is true that the prospect of bankruptcy or the loss of a job can concentrate the mind wonderfully, and lead some people to work harder and better. But the need to put this sort of pressure on the firms and industries that need to decline, or else to improve their efficiency greatly, should not be confused with the very different policy of holding down economic activity *generally* – which is the very *opposite* of the sort of macroeconomic policy that is required to bring about desirable forms of structural adjustment and improvements in efficiency. Indeed, in a recession many of the least economic industries receive some sort of support – by subsidies or protection against imports – which *slows down* the necessary structural adjustment; for governments can be more readily prevailed upon to help an industry in difficulties when there are no jobs available elsewhere for those who would otherwise have had to leave the industry. A policy that sought to achieve speedy and efficient structural adjustment would thus be the exact antithesis of that which has generally prevailed in the developed world during the 1970s: it would be to maintain full employment – maximising the job opportunities for people released from contracting firms and industries – but placing the maximum of downward pressure on demand for uneconomic industries, by reducing or removing as speedily as possible the various forms of assistance that have been accorded to such industries. A *general* 'shake-out' of industry is likely also to play havoc with those industries that ought to be expanding; indeed, many of the industries that ought to be expanding may not even come into existence if the macroeconomic policies that are pursued are ones that prevent full employment.

Whatever the arguments may be for tolerating high unemployment (and this book has made it clear that the author does not share them) they do not include the argument that recession can help to effect desirable forms of structural adjustment. Indeed, by fostering protectionism deflationary policies will postpone or prevent the necessary forms of adjustment. This adjustment can far more efficiently be achieved by steady, pre-announced, reductions in all forms of assistance to less economic industries combined with macroeconomic policies that ensure there are an adequate number of jobs to absorb those released from the declining industries.

TAX CUTS AND RESOURCE ALLOCATION

If one believes that a particular form of tax cuts would have undesirable effects on the allocation of resources, this is clearly an argument for choosing another form of tax cut. There are certainly no grounds for believing that the types of tax cuts that would do most to cut costs and prices would be ones that would have *adverse* effects on resource allocation – and the presumption is that the sort of tax cuts that did most to improve the allocation of resources would also contribute most to cutting costs. But one can safely say that probably all taxes have some cost-increasing effects, and we do not really know which have the greatest upward effect on costs and prices.

If one has resource-allocation objectives that conflict with macroeconomic objectives, naturally this may involve a particular pattern of taxes and subsidies with no unique advantage from a macro point of view; many alternative patterns could be more or less effective for the achievement of macroeconomic goals, but only if the package in question does not appreciably reduce real output per head. Nevertheless, a resource-allocation policy that minimises pollution (for example) may well prejudice the achievement of macroeconomic goals by raising costs; if so, obviously the government has to choose what weight to give to each objective.

In any case, so long as the economy is operating appreciably below its economic potential, the macroeconomic policy that does most to return it towards full capacity operation with the minimum of additional upward pressure on prices is likely also to do most to increase economic welfare. If by any chance the macroeconomic policy in question worsened the allocation of resources *at any given level of activity* (which is the criterion on which resource-allocation policies are usually judged) it is difficult to imagine a case where the welfare gain on that score would justify continuing to operate the economy at well below full employment, rather than using an appropriate mix, accompanied by an appropriate form of stimulus, to reduce or to stop stagflation.

THE POLICY MIX AND ECONOMIC GROWTH

The degree of success with which the economy achieves full employment is probably the most important influence on the rate of economic growth and the level of real output in any particular year. The adoption of a less inflationary mix would be the best way to reduce or remove the temptation for governments to tolerate high unemployment in the hope of thereby checking the upward pressure on prices: and this would do much to restore a high rate of economic growth.

There are, however, other influences that affect the overall level of real output and its rate of growth *at any given level of employment*. One of these is the level of investment that takes place at each level of employment, and another is the efficiency with which resources generally are allocated. Both of these may be affected by the choice of macroeconomic measures.

The standard accepted analysis in the past has been that a mix with easy money and high taxes will lead to a higher level of investment than its opposite, and that this will be 'good for growth'. But this view is highly suspect, and is likely to be the very opposite of the truth if one starts from a situation of stagflation in which the government is tolerating high unemployment in the hope of checking inflation.

For there is *no* good reason to assume that the *ratio* of productive investment to total output will be reduced by cutting taxes and tightening monetary policy. In the first place, this change of mix might well tend to raise the propensity to save – that is, to reduce the ratio of consumption to total output; and the net result would be determined by its impact on *both* saving decisions *and* investment decisions.

Secondly, 'investment' in the standard models is defined as meaning *all* those outlays that are affected by interest rates rather than (or not merely) by the level of income. In developed countries these include many types of consumer outlays – including dwelling construction, which is probably more responsive to interest rate changes than is fixed investment by businesses. Expenditure on consumer durables, especially motor vehicles, is also likely to be influenced by credit conditions and monetary policy; and outlays on consumer durables, largely financed by borrowing, may well be among the categories of outlay most affected by interest rates. These outlays are also influenced by the level of dwelling construction, as many such goods are purchased to equip new dwellings. In some countries mortgage interest payments are tax deductible, and sometimes (as in the USA) even interest payments on credit borrowed to finance spending on consumer durables. Where this is true, one important effect of a shift to higher interest rates and lower tax rates is likely to be a reduction in the share of consumer-durables expenditure in total demand.

Furthermore, some studies have suggested that outlays by business on fixed investment are *not* especially sensitive to interest-rate changes; but they are probably far more sensitive to the prospects of profitable sales – which means that so long as recession continues investment will be depressed, but a higher level of activity made possible by a better macroeconomic mix would be likely to raise investment.

The foregoing considerations add up to a strong case against the orthodox view that a mix with low interest rates and high taxes will mainly encourage productive investment. But much depends on which taxes would be cut – or which subsidies increased – if the opposite mix of lower taxes and tight money were adopted. It would certainly be possible to cut taxes (or increase subsidies) in a manner that would give a considerable stimulus to productive forms of investment.

But even if the net result were a reduction in the proportion of investment to total output, there could still be a rise in the absolute level of investment (at any given level of employment) if the shift to tighter monetary policies and lower taxes had very favourable effects on productivity, so that all forms of output and outlay could be higher in real terms. Favourable productivity effects could occur both because the tax reduction itself improved productivity and because the capital market began to operate more efficiently when interest rates after tax were no longer very low (or negative).

Moreover, even if the level of *investment* were not actually higher at that level of employment, total real *output* could still be higher if the productivity effects of the tax cuts were sufficiently favourable.

But the main reason why a shift to a mix with lower taxes and tighter monetary policy may be expected to lead to faster growth, and probably also to a higher absolute level of productive investment, is that the downward pressure that such a shift of mix will exert on prices should make the government less inclined to tolerate high unemployment, so that the general level of both employment and real output will be higher under this mix than under its opposite. The best way of stimulating growth is to stop stagflation. If a superficial concern that a policy of tight money and low taxes might reduce the ratio of investment to total output stands in the way of such a mix (as it appears to in some people's minds) it is important to correct this view as quickly as possible.

If some other mix of macroeconomic measures was preferable from the viewpoint of achieving an ideal ratio of investment to output, that preferred mix could be substituted once full employment was restored; it must always be preferable in the interim to adopt a mix that will minimise inflation *without* the loss of output, or the social suffering, resulting from a temporarily high level of unemployment. Under a mix that maintains something closer to full employment in the short run, it is, moreover, likely that a higher absolute level of investment will occur even if its ratio to total output is lower.

Does investment reduce prices?

There is, however, an inevitable conflict between the short-run advantages of devoting a high proportion *of any given level of output* to consumption and the longer-run advantages of devoting a higher proportion to productive investment. For the greater the proportion of output that is used to produce consumption goods in the near future, the less is likely to be the upward pressure on the price level of consumption goods during that period, and the easier it is therefore likely to be to hold down money wage demands over the same period. On the other hand, if more is devoted to productive investment in the near future, this will make possible a higher level of output of consumption goods in the longer run, and thus reduce the upward pressure on prices in future. The ideal proportion of investment to total output will therefore depend partly on how severe the upward pressure on prices is at present, and how severe it is thought likely to be in future; and partly on the relative weight we give to the need to check inflation now compared with the need to restrain it in future.

Policy conclusions relating to investment

The tax-cut element in the package to stop stagflation can be applied in various ways, which will give varying degrees of stimulus to investment (relative to consumption). The overall tax structure should, in any event, be constantly revised to ensure that it is not holding down productive investment unduly. But the general macroeconomic case for tight monetary policy and low tax rates is not weakened by these considerations – which relate to the tax *structure*, rather than to the overall level of taxation.

A mix involving low tax rates (especially in forms that would encourage productive investment and saving) coupled with an appropriately tight monetary policy could be expected to encourage investment by reducing inflation at any given level of employment, and thus making governments readier to permit the restoration of full employment. The misplaced fear that tighter monetary policies coupled with tax cuts might adversely affect investment appeared to be (at the start of the 1980s) a psychological obstacle to the implementation of an appropriate mix for stopping stagflation – even though the simplistic models on which such a prejudice appeared to be based are throughly misleading as to the relative effects of the mix in question on the ratio of productive investment to consumption, and are not useful as guides to this aspect of macroeconomic policies in a situation of stagflation.

PROTECTION AGAINST MANUFACTURED IMPORTS FROM THE LESS DEVELOPED COUNTRIES

Probably the most conspicuous form of protectionism that has adverse effects on both those countries that are applying it and on the rest of the world is the extensive range of tariffs, import controls, and so-called 'voluntary restraints' on the flow of manufactures such as textiles from the less developed (but industrialising) countries of the world into the rich countries. These limitations have intensified during the recession of the 1970s. They are obviously damaging to those countries that can economically export such goods. They also affect adversely consumers in the rich countries; and so far as the consequent upward pressure on the prices at which such goods can be purchased in the rich countries makes governments more inclined to tolerate high unemployment, it makes recession worse in the rich countries. One can understand the political force of the producer lobbies that ask for such assistance; but it would be in the interests of all countries if assistance to these individuals were in forms that enabled them to leave the industry unless they can rationalise their production in a way that makes them competitive. At the same time, however, it is essential for the governments of rich countries to maintain a level of employment that ensures that resources of manpower released from such industries are quickly absorbed elsewhere.

THE COMMON AGRICULTURAL POLICY OF THE EUROPEAN ECONOMIC COMMUNITY

The Common Agricultural Policy (the 'CAP') of the EEC is another form of a resource-allocation policy that has especially conspicuous adverse macroeconomic (as well as resource allocation) effects both on the countries applying it and on the world as a whole. It is a highly complex system for protecting agricultural production in Western Europe, and it operates in ways that are especially likely to have adverse effects on economic welfare and on the achievement of macroeconomic policy objectives. No government that was genuinely and seriously concerned with stopping stagflation could logically adhere to the CAP in anything like its present form.

The essence of the CAP is that it supports the prices received by agricultural producers in Western Europe, and that it does so by holding up the prices paid by consumers in Western Europe above the level at which they would be in a free market. It does this by various forms of limitations, including import levies, on imports of agricultural products from outside the EEC, and by building up large stocks of many agricultural products within Europe ('butter mountains', 'wine lakes' and so on), and by a considerable amount of subsidies on the export of various products (sugar, for example), which adversely affect the markets of more economic producers of these commodities outside the EEC.

Not only does this policy result in various types of food production being encouraged in an area where most of the production is less economic, and discouraged in other countries where it is more economic (New Zealand, being an extreme example), but the method whereby assistance is given to Europe's agricultural industry is in forms that raise the price of these basic items of consumption to the consumer, in contrast to the less uneconomic method of subsidising the prices received by producers (the latter being the method used by Britain before she entered the EEC).

The consequently higher prices of these items is of fundamental importance in the household budgets of everyone in the EEC, and it presumably makes wage demands (and other income demands) higher than they would otherwise have been. In view of the importance of foodstuffs in all consumer price indexes, this implies that a reform of the CAP, either in the direction of giving less support to uneconomic producers of foodstuffs, or in the form of giving the same degree of assistance in ways that avoid the upward pressure on food prices, could exert a considerable downward impact on the price level, and so on the rate of inflation during the relevant period provided that the producer subsidies were not financed by the creation of money, and especially if they were financed by borrowing from the non-bank public.

The CAP in anything like its present form thus makes it more difficult for the governments of member countries to check the rise in the price level. If they then react to this situation by tolerating more unemployment than they would otherwise have done, this naturally reacts unfavourably on the incomes of agricultural producers, and so increases the level of assistance to them that is necessary in order to provide them with a given real income. This is thus clearly another form of a stagflationary and resource-allocation vicious circle.

If the CAP had favourable effects on the rest of the world sufficient to counterbalance its adverse effects on the EEC countries, it might be defended from a global point of view. It certainly has some favourable effects on some purchasers of foodstuffs on concessional terms from the EEC – including Russians and Poles (in certain years), as well as in some less developed countries. But it has adverse effects on more economic food producers (most obviously in New Zealand, but to some extent also in Canada, Australia and the USA) including some in the less developed countries of the world, whose sugar and vegetable-oil exports are adversely affected by the EEC's support for its beet-sugar producers and butter producers. Clearly, this makes it harder for the countries where these more economic producers are located to solve their macroeconomic problems, in addition to the problems it presents for macroeconomic policy within the EEC itself. It seems unlikely that any favourable effects that operate through holding down food prices in poor food-importing countries that may benefit from it (at least temporarily) would constitute an appreciable offset to these adverse macroeconomic effects from the viewpoint of the world as a whole.

But concessional food exports are generally an inefficient form of aid, though this may well be because it is misused by the recipient governments so as to delay improvements to their own agriculture; and if so, the remedy is in their hands – so that this does not constitute a conclusive case for cutting food aid. But the *indirect* unfavourable effects on food-importing countries – through consequent reductions in the availability of food from countries (such as New Zealand) that could have exported it more cheaply to them over the long run – have to be set on the other side. The likelihood that cheap-food aid from the EEC will be only temporary and will disappear when the food mountains subside (when a reform of the CAP becomes inevitable, as it presumably will do eventually) also makes it an inefficient form of aid to poorer countries, which will subsequently have to improve their own agriculture when this temporary aid is reduced.

On balance, therefore, it would be very difficult to argue convincingly that any helpful effects that the CAP may have on developing countries that obtain cheap food as a result of it would go far towards offsetting the undoubtedly adverse effects it has on the EEC countries themselves and on the more economic producers in the rest of the world.

MACROECONOMIC POLICY AND MAKE-WORK REMEDIES FOR UNEMPLOYMENT

In periods when unemployment is high there are usually proposals for making the level of unemployment appear to be less – by sharing the work around, by employing people on government relief works of types that would not otherwise have been undertaken, by introducing shorter working weeks, early retirement and so on. The recent period of high unemployment in the western world has seen some considerable resort to such policies, and widespread discussion of them.

The later 1970s, in particular, saw two important new considerations arise that had a bearing on the use of make-work remedies for unemployment. One of these was the technological advances that raised productivity *in certain industries*, mainly those industries that were able to make good use of the rapid developments in microelectronics, especially as this was in a period when the *general* level of productivity in the western world was *not* rising rapidly. Indeed, the rate of productivity increase *slowed down* considerably in the 1970s, at a time when productivity increases in the electronic industries were being applied widely in many occupations.

The other main feature of this recent period when make-work remedies for unemployment were widely discussed, and to some extent implemented, is that the high unemployment was accompanied by high rates of inflation. Any make-work remedy for unemployment will normally make it harder to hold down the price level; and this meant that the widespread policies of trying to tackle inflation by creating more unemployment actually caused the 'make-work' remedies for unemployment to be counter-productive; for they tended to *raise* unemployment when account is taken of their indirect effects through government policy reactions to the consequent upward pressure on the price level.

The essence of make-work 'remedies' for unemployment

The characteristic of all 'make-work' remedies (or, rather, *supposed* remedies) for unemployment is that they increase the amount of effort that the community has to apply in order to achieve a given level of real output; in other words, they decrease the aggregate real income that can be achieved with a given input of economic effort. The less efficiently an economy is run, the more jobs there must be to achieve a given real output. A very large number of jobs could be created (in certain industries) by replacing bulldozers by men working with teaspoons. But this does not imply that less efficient methods of production will increase the *total* number of jobs; for any such conclusion would depend on the quite unrealistic assumption that there is a fixed quantity of real output that has be produced, and that neither more nor less than that output will be produced, irrespective of the methods used. Clearly, that would be an absurd proposition, for in fact the use of the more efficient methods is normally applied to increase real living standards, and so to make it possible for the same number of jobs to be available with a

Resource Allocation Policy and Macroeconomic Policy 103

higher real output per head. But it is also possible for the use of *in*efficient methods to be accompanied by a net *decline* in the number of jobs — and that has almost certainly been the effect of the adoption of relatively inefficient methods of production during a period when governments were reacting to inflation by permitting higher levels of unemployment.

The most obvious form of make-work remedy is the delaying of technological progress — which has been called 'latter-day Luddism' (after the Luddites' machinery-smashing, motivated by a desire to maintain jobs in the textile industries, in early nineteenth-century Britain). The normal course of economic progress has been for less efficient methods to be replaced by more efficient methods, thereby enabling consumers to enjoy higher living standards — which may or may not imply higher outputs in the particular industries where productive efficiency has increased. Workers who may lose their jobs as a result of technological advances, cannot usually tell in advance (or even in retrospect) whether the eventual effect will be a proportionately greater consumption of the products of the industry or firm in which they are employed. Nor do they know whether or not they will obtain jobs elsewhere. Sometimes they are merely reacting against the need to move, or to change their work, or retrain. It is often said that, as technological advance proceeds in the modern world, people are likely to have to change their work several times in a working lifetime. In any event, there is no doubt that the rate of economic progress is greatest when people are ready to change their work according to changes in productive methods and other factors (such as consumer tastes), and that it is consequently less when countries and individuals (and unions and employers) resist such necessary changes.

When unemployment is high, inducements are often given to people to retire early. This is the same sort of waste of useful productive potential as paying the unemployed to remain idle; for it generally increases the demands made on the available output of goods and services (or, more exactly, it increases the *net* demand for them by giving the unemployed, or the retired, income to spend when they are not producing anything, or not as much as they would have done if in normal employment). In this sense, both policies imply the belief that there is a fixed stock of goods and services to be produced, and which will be produced in any case, irrespective of whether the people in question are lost to the work force. But, of course, a moment's thought will suffice to show that this need not be so. The adoption of an appropriate macroeconomic policy — or even policies that permitted the market system to do its job properly — would enable these people to produce useful goods and services of types that they and others would like to buy. Only if it were true that people's wants have already been fully satisfied (which they manifestly have not) would it make any sense to regard work as a privilege to be rationed out among those ready or eager to perform it. This is not an objection to early retirement when it is *voluntary*, and is accepted in the knowledge that the individual concerned will consequently obtain a proportionately smaller retirement pension (which fully reflects his or her reduced contribution – after retirement – to the community's output of useful goods and services). Similarly, if people who are employed choose to work shorter hours in a day or week, *and also agree to accept correspondingly lower remuneration* to offset their lower real output, this will presumably be adding to their economic welfare. But if shorter hours are encouraged as a result of a muddled view that high unemployment makes it necessary to share the available work, this is a further example of 'make-work' remedies for unemployment – in the sense that it reduces productive efficiency, by reducing the community's ability to satisfy people's wants, and thus tends to force up prices.

An especially dangerous form of this is when calls for a shorter working week are merely disguised forms of wage and salary increases. For if they mean mainly that a larger proportion of the working week is paid at overtime rates, they thereby place additional upward pressure on prices; and even if they do result in shorter hours being worked, but if incomes are not cut fully in proportion to any consequent fall in output, again there would be upward pressure on the price level. (It is of course possible that shorter working hours – in some forms – can actually increase output; and where this is so, this change should be advocated in any case; it certainly would not then be a 'make-work' remedy for unemployment, because it would be *increasing* productive efficiency. But this should certainly not be confused with the sort of shorter working week which merely means a rise in the proportion of the working week paid for as overtime – which can only make prices higher.)

The effect on total employment of a rise in productivity in a particular industry or firm is *not* usually apparent to any of those affected. Any rise in employment that may subsequently occur elsewhere (or in the industry concerned) cannot in practice be traced with any certainty to the improvement in productivity, despite the fact that the rise in real incomes that it brings about will lead people to increase their consumption of goods and services eventually, except so far as they choose leisure instead.

If it could be assumed that full employment would automatically be maintained, there would obviously be no cause for concern and presumably no one would then make a case for 'make-work' remedies. People would then decide whether they prefer more goods and services or more leisure, and whether they prefer to work (for their current income or a lower one), or whether they would prefer more leisure; and the market mechanism would give effect to these preferences. If, on the other hand, one takes the view that the market mechanism does not automatically ensure full employment, one must argue that the government ought to take appropriate steps to maintain full employment in the face of the rise in productivity – so far as this does not occur automatically. This will not be more difficult to achieve if the community takes advantage of the available potential rises in productivity to enable it to produce the goods and services that people want as efficiently as possible. Indeed, as argued above, when there is a rapid rise in productivity this makes it easier to keep inflation under control (and the slowing down in the rate of productivity increase in the 1970s made it harder to do so); so that those governments that believe unemployment will help to check inflation are consequently more likely to tolerate higher unemployment if the available potential increases in productivity are *not* applied whenever possible.

The role of macroeconomic policy is crucial in determining whether or not people will be prepared to change their employment. For reluctance to accept the need for change is clearly greatest when jobs are most difficult to obtain in new industries or by new forms of productive activity in existing industries. In this context, the modern heresy (in some countries) that high unemployment *promotes* technological change is especially dangerous. It is true that it may 'shake out' employees from the old and declining industries (among others), but it denies most of them the opportunity to produce something useful elsewhere. It is a perhaps understandable over-reaction to earlier policies of 'overfull employment', and to the excessive assistance granted to many industries that should have declined. But the right remedy would have been to remove the assistance to the declining industries, whilst simultaneously ensuring that employment was 'full' enough to ensure that people can readily find places where they can do new forms of productive work. By contrast, the recent policies of deflation coupled with the protection of many industries that ought to decline has produced the worst of all these possible worlds: high unemployment and inflation coupled with gross misallocation of resources.

CONCLUSIONS

Economic growth in the world economy, and in any individual country, depends on (1) how fully the available resources are utilised (that is, on how successfully full employment is maintained); and (2) how efficiently and economically resources are allocated among the various possible uses of them at the prevailing level of employment.

The main theme of this chapter is that the choice of a combination of macroeconomic policy measures that maintains a high level of employment with a minimum of upward pressure on the price level will make it easier to reduce or remove uneconomic forms of protection and other forms of assistance to particular industries, and will also reduce the risk of the adoption of 'make-work' remedies for unemployment. Moreover, the improvement in the efficiency with which a country utilises its available resources (at any given level of employment) will influence its macroeconomic policies; for an improvement in the use of its resources that results from reducing uneconomic forms of assistance to particular industries exerts a downward effect on prices, and will thus reduce the risk that governments will feel tempted to try to check inflation by maintaining unemployment at a high level. The many forms of limitations upon imports are among the ways in which productivity and economic welfare are reduced (for the world as a whole) during periods when there is considerable unemployment; and this tends to hold up prices (at the prevailing level of unemployment). This means that a general reduction in the barriers to trade will make it easier for inflation to be held in check, and so make governments less disposed to tolerate high unemployment. By the same token, if unemployment is reduced, governments are less likely to impose additional barriers to trade, and more likely to reduce the existing ones.

The best way of ensuring that resources move towards those forms of production where they can be put to good use is for governments to adopt both macroeconomic and resource-allocation policies that would be virtually the opposite of those that have generally prevailed in recent years. That is to say, governments ought to be placing as much pressure as possible upon the least economic industries to contract, whilst simultaneously ensuring that the overall level of employment in the economy is such that people who lose their jobs in declining regions and industries can readily find jobs elsewhere. By contrast, the policies of most governments in the late 1970s and early 1980s have been to protect many of those industries that had the most adverse long-run economic prospects (at least, those among them that were important employers of labour), whilst keeping the general level of unemployment high.

It is curious that those economists who have been most vocal in support of the view that market forces ought to play the major role in determining the allocation of resources among industries, and that government assistance for uneconomic industries should therefore be reduced or removed as quickly as possible, have usually been also among those who have been most vocal in advocating deflationary policies as a means of tackling inflation: yet the adoption of macroeconomic policies of that sort made it correspondingly harder to bring about the elimination of uneconomic forms of protection and the relocation of the resources thus released into more economic industries.

The maintenance of a high level of employment (by non-inflationary means) could also be expected to encourage a high level of productive investment. This would help to hold down inflation in future, though it may increase the upward pressure on consumer prices in the present. The inefficiencies that result from 'make-work' remedies (so-called) for unemployment are bound to reduce living standards, raise prices, and consequently make governments more inclined to tolerate a high general level of unemployment, in the hope that it will hold down price increases. They can thus only make the problem of stagflation worse.

7 Criticisms, Complications and Conclusions

This final chapter first considers criticisms that some might wish to make of proposals along the lines of those put forward in earlier chapters. It is pointed out that the present proposals are consistent with the use of prices and incomes policies (so far as such policies may be feasible), but that no prices and incomes policy will be likely to succeed unless it is complemented by due attention to the appropriate mix of macroeconomic measures. Some of the principal political obstacles to making proper use of the mix to stop stagflation are outlined, and some concluding observations are made on certain general issues.

PROBLEMS AND PSEUDO-OBJECTIONS

There are a number of points that people have raised in commenting on policy proposals on the lines of those made in this book; and these deserve to be set down and answered.

'Taxes may not be very cost-inflationary'

Provided that taxes have *some* cost-inflationary effect that is not shared by either reductions in some forms of government spending (as a ratio of total output) or by a tightening of monetary policy, the general argument for a switch of mix in one of the forms involving tax cuts is valid. Those who doubt whether taxes have much cost-inflationary effect have been known to put this point as if it were an objection to the mixes in question; but in fact it is simply an argument for making rather larger tax reductions (and correspondingly larger changes in the other instrument or instruments).

The only circumstances in which that policy might not be beneficial would be if a greater switch of the mix carried large net disadvantages that were not to be expected when there was only a smaller switch; but the disadvantages would have to be on such a scale as to exceed the benefit of being

Criticisms, Complications and Conclusions 109

consequently able to avoid the use of the alternative policy of higher unemployment. In fact, however, the favourable resource-allocation effects that could be expected from generally lower taxes and (reliably) positive real post-tax interest rates for lenders would have *helpful* resource-allocation effects (even if they had no helpful macroeconomic effects). It would, by contrast, be necessary to adduce good grounds for believing that a large switch of mix would have considerable and clear *disadvantages* if the need to make relatively large tax cuts were to be a valid objection to making use of such a mix (rather than tolerating high unemployment). Moreover, if those disadvantages were of a sort that made it harder to solve the macroeconomic problem of stagflation it would simply mean that the optimal mix would then become a switch of the mix in the opposite direction.

'Won't some temporary unemployment still be necessary?'

The comment has been made that a temporarily high level of unemployment will still be necessary: that a switch of mix can do no more than minimise the amount of temporarily high unemployment required to reduce the rate of inflation by a given amount. But if a *small* switch of mix will have some effect in bringing down the rate of inflation over the relevant period, and if this would otherwise have been achieved by enduring more unemployment, then a *larger* switch of mix ought to make it possible to avoid the need for any unemployment at all for this purpose. The only valid argument against this view would be if the switch of mix in question could be shown to have social and economic costs as great as those of the unemployment. But as the costs of the unemployment and the waste of potential output (that result from the alternative policy) are certain, any such counter-argument would need to be established very convincingly. Certainly, nothing like the current policies that involve tolerating unemployment (rather than a change of mix) for this purpose could reasonably be defended without first addressing, and then convincingly establishing, the view that this mix would have more than offsetting real costs to set on the other side. In fact, however, the favourable productivity effects and the more efficient operation of the capital market that could be expected to result from a more appropriate mix would be worth having in themselves, so that it is more likely that there would be net non-macroeconomic *benefits* from the switch of mix than that there would be net costs to set on the other side. Those who say that a big enough switch to avoid the need for some temporarily high unemployment is not desirable usually have in mind some pseudo-target for the budget deficit which they fear will be exceeded if a mix were adopted to stop stagflation without temporarily high unemployment; and they assume that the only mix that would work would be one that would increase the budget deficit – which is, in any case, not necessarily true.

'What if you can't sell the bonds?'

The proposal to cut taxes and sell bonds is often met with the objection that 'it may not be possible to sell enough bonds'. This objection seems to spring from the implicit assumption that there is some fixed target for the quantity of money that has to be achieved irrespective of the level of employment or of the mix of measures with which it is achieved, and some fixed quantity of bonds that can be sold (irrespective of their price). But the quantity of money that is desirable depends upon the level of real output and on the price level at which it can be achieved, as well as on the combination of macroeconomic measures that is being employed: whilst the quantity of bonds that can be sold depends on the price at which they are offered and the disposable incomes of the public to whom the bonds are being sold. The aim of macro policy should be to re-establish full employment without inflation by choosing the combination of measures to bring about the desired level of employment that is most likely to have least upward effect on the price level. It is unnecessary and harmful to superimpose upon this approach to policy a relic of the discredited approach that consists of thinking of a target for the rate of growth of the quantity of money, or for the budget deficit, or for (nominal) GDP, and then trying to achieve it without paying due attention to the combination of measures by which it is achieved. For there is no reason to suppose that any particular target for some chosen monetary aggregate (or for the budget deficit) will turn out to be consistent with employing the mix of instruments that will be most appropriate for achieving the best available approximation to the macroeconomic objectives. The whole purpose of concentrating on the *real* macro objectives is to *avoid* being dominated by monetary or budgetary targets that are highly unlikely to be consistent with the real aims of macroeconomic policy.

But, in fact, a government that attempts to deal with stagflation by cutting taxes and selling bonds – without simultaneously setting itself interest rate or monetary targets – will be *more* likely to keep the growth of the quantity of money under reasonable control than one that sets itself a monetary target and then tries to achieve it by means of excessive tax rates coupled with low or negative real post-tax interest rates (which make it very difficult to keep the quantity of money under control). For bonds are difficult to sell principally when governments try to resist the market forces that are pulling interest rates up; and it is much harder to hold down the rate of increase in any monetary aggregate when monetary policy is being kept relatively easy and

Criticisms, Complications and Conclusions   111

when tax rates are at high levels, both of which tend to increase costs and prices and to cause high levels of borrowing from banks. So far from the proposed mix of lower taxes and relatively tight monetary policies making it *less* likely that sufficient bonds will be sold, it is therefore likely to reduce or remove the main obstacles to adequate sales of government securities, especially if a wide range of alternative index-linked securities is being offered to the public; and it is likely also to make it easier to keep the volume of money under control, by holding down borrowing from banks – and so reducing the amount of bonds that *needs* to be sold in order to hold down the quantity of money to any particular figure.

'Will a switch of mix have a lasting effect on inflation?'

Some critics of the proposal to use a switch of mix – instead of policies that cause higher unemployment – to restrain inflation have said that the effect of the former will be only 'once for all'. It is true that there is likely to be a greater dampening effect on inflation over the period of the change of mix than there will be over the longer run: but exactly the same can be said of the effect of a temporarily high level of unemployment. If it were really true that a 'once-for-all' effect in reducing inflation were not worth having, that would also be an objection to achieving it by means of temporarily high unemployment. But governments would (and should) always welcome a once-for-all improvement (provided at least that it was not subsequently actually *reversed*): and the switch of mix would achieve it without the loss of output and other social costs associated with temporarily high unemployment; and this would obviously be preferable from both a political and an economic viewpoint. Only if a switch of mix had some seriously adverse long-run effects on posterity (not shared by the alternative) would there be a case for tolerating temporarily high unemployment instead.

But, in fact, posterity will be *better* off if we stop stagflation quickly, rather than operating the economy below capacity for a 'temporary' period. For the stock of human and material capital available to posterity will be correspondingly greater if the unemployment is avoided and output in the interim is therefore higher. As output per head will therefore also be higher – and the price level to that extent lower – in future if the short-term unemployment is avoided, this should bring down the actual and expected rate of inflation (between the present and the future year in question) by more than if we had relied on high unemployment to achieve the same short-run effect.

Those who prefer the use of policies that involve high unemployment in the near future would therefore need to establish that a check to inflation brought about in that way would have more lasting effects in bringing down the expected and actual rate of inflation. But there is no reasonable likelihood that this would be so. For success in bringing down inflation depends to some extent on the confidence of the public that the government will persist in its anti-inflationary policies: and the public would be unlikely to believe for long in the government's determination to persevere with policies that were causing unemployment; whereas they would be far more likely to believe that it would continue (especially as an election approached) to pursue a policy that kept unemployment (and tax rates) low, whilst having the same effect on the price level over the period in question.

Moreover, if it were really true that some of the reduction in the rates of inflation could be achieved *only* by high unemployment, that effect would vanish when unemployment started to fall. In that case, it would thus be impossible for the advocates of such policies to continue to assert that low levels of unemployment could subsequently be restored without a return to higher inflation.

A tax cut that reduced price increases over the period of the change could be expected to have at least some downward impact on the expected rate of inflation. Even if it were true that this effect on inflationary expectations was less (for a given fall in the rate of inflation over the period of the switch of mix) than it would have been if the same effect on inflation over that period had been achieved by a temporarily high level of unemployment, that would simply mean that a correspondingly larger switch of mix would then be required (so as to have a correspondingly greater downward impact on the rate of inflation over the period of the switch of mix) in order to have a given lasting impact on the expected rate of inflation. Only if there were *no* lasting downward impact on the expected rate of inflation after an appropriate switch of mix would that weaken the argument for using a switch of mix for that purpose.

Critics of the use of a switch of mix for reducing inflation have been known to suggest that *repeated* switches of the mix would be necessary to have this effect. But if that were true, a continued high level of unemployment would also be necessary (under the alternative policies) to have a lasting effect on inflation. In fact, however, either a temporary rise in unemployment or a single switch of mix would operate also on inflationary expectations so far as it reduced the rise in prices experienced over some period.

It is true that such shifts cannot be repeated indefinitely. But the proposal is to correct an excessive shift in the *wrong* direction that occurred in most countries during the 1970s (and to a lesser extent in earlier years) as illustrated in Tables 2.2 and 2.3 in Chapter 2. It is therefore not reasonable to suppose that the shift would need to be repeated indefinitely.

There is, in any case, one respect in which an appropriate switch of mix may well reduce also the underlying rate of inflation over the longer period (even apart from the effects on expectations). If (as seems likely) the high rates of taxation in the 1970s gave rise to inconsistent income claims by employers and employees, a cut in tax rates generally could therefore be expected to leave both sides of industry more satisfied with any given pre-tax income (and so less likely to bid against one another in a manner that forced up both prices and wages).[1] A once-for-all cut in tax rates (whether accompanied by lower government outlays or tighter monetary policies) may thus have some lasting effect on the underlying rate of inflation, even if the dose of tax cuts were not repeated, and even apart from effects through expectations. Once the setting of instruments was brought back to something like that which was usual in the 1960s, the problem of stagflation might well have been solved.

'Real wages are too high'

The analysis of the foregoing chapters has implicitly taken the view that the *real* wage problem is not the *real-wage* problem, but the *money-wage* problem. In other words, that the crucial step towards stopping stagflation is to check the rise in money wages *and* other *nominal* incomes – rather than to reduce the rate of increase in wages *relative to prices or profits*.

But this is not intended to deny that there was in the middle of the 1970s a tendency in many countries (though not in the USA) for the share of real wages in total incomes to rise 'too high' relative to profits, in the sense that *at current tax rates* the real level of profits available to employers after tax was insufficient (given current real wages) to make it worth while for them to provide the jobs that were needed if full employment was to be restored. In this situation, most forms of expansionary measures would probably have led to more rapid inflation, rather than higher employment; but for most (if not all) countries this situation seems to have passed by the end of the 1970s.

In any case, this leaves open the question of how far the difficulty arose *because of excessively high tax rates* and how far it was due to a *relative rise in wage rates* (compared with non-wage incomes). For an analysis in terms of wages and profits only is not helpful when governments are appropriating a large slice of the national cake through taxation and using so much of the available resources to make possible high levels of government outlay. If the problem is one of an excessive level of consumption – relative to investment and other forms of claim on the national resources – this should be met by measures to restrain consumption, and to facilitate higher levels of investment. If the view is that the high level of wage-costs, relative to the prices that employers can obtain for their goods, is making it unprofitable for them to employ more labour, this can be true only for the given level of taxation (in all forms) that employers are paying. This means that either a cut in those taxes or a reduction in the (real) wage rates that they are paying is necessary to encourage them to provide more employment.

It is important to distinguish, on the one hand, *real wages as a cost* to employers — for which pre-tax wage rates, and the prices received by the employers for their products, are the relevant factors; and, on the other hand, *real wages as an income* — for which the post-tax wages received by employees and the prices of the goods they buy (some of which are imported, and not produced by those who employ them) are the relevant magnitudes. A cut in the taxes paid by wage-earners may have some effect in restraining wage increases; and so far as this occurs it can reduce real wages as a cost to employers whilst actually increasing real wages as an income (in post-tax terms) to the employee. Of course, the tax cuts will have to be financed in some way, and it is true that the accompanying monetary measures, or even some forms of cuts in government spending, may tend to raise the costs of employers to some greater or smaller extent. But this does not alter the fact that real wages as a cost (especially if one takes account of wage-related taxes and other payments such as social-services contributions paid by employers, or payroll taxes) are a very different matter from real wages as an income (in the sense of what the employee can buy with them). Governments that were arguing in the 1970s that real wages were too high (a 'real-wage overhang') might just as well have said that tax rates were too high. It was seldom asked how far the right remedy was tax cuts rather than reductions in the rate of increase in real wage rates. (One never heard mention of a 'real-*tax* overhang'.) But there can be no reasonable doubt that *nominal* incomes, including money-wage rates, were rising too fast (partly because taxes were high) — and that this was a main reason why stagflation was so hard to stop.

Moreover, the sharp rise in money wage rates (leading to increases in real wage rates) in many OECD countries did not occur until about 1973, whereas (as we saw in Chapter 2) the problem of stagflation began in the later 1960s, and, when it did occur, it is reasonable to trace it partly to the rise in tax rates and the fall in real interest rates that had been occurring by then for about half a decade. In any case, as there was no rise in the general level of real-wage shares in the USA, this factor cannot be invoked to account for any part of the stagflation of the mid-1970s in the largest OECD country.

By the end of the 1970s, it could reasonably be said that throughout most of the OECD world the 'real' wage problem was not the *real-wage*, problem, but the *money-wage* problem (provided that this is understood as referring to excessive rises in money incomes generally).[2]

THE MIX AND PRICES AND INCOMES POLICIES

Some of those who favour the use of some sort of prices and incomes policy have been less than enthusiastic about using an appropriate mix of macroeconomic instruments to stop stagflation. Yet incomes policies are perfectly compatible with a proper use of the mix; and, indeed, are unlikely to succeed if the mix employed is one tending to raise prices.

The foregoing proposals to minimise the upward pressure on prices (at any given level of employment), by choosing an appropriate macroeconomic mix, are in fact consistent with a very wide variety of viewpoints about the desirability and feasibility of some sort of prices and incomes policy (including those that operate by providing tax incentives to hold down prices and money wage increases).

Governments always exert some influence over certain prices and incomes – even if only the prices they charge for goods and services that they sell and the wages and salaries they pay in the public sector. Moreover, if they allow public sector pay to rise rapidly, this will usually have an indirect upward effect on wage and salary settlements in the private sector also. To allow antipathy towards certain types of incomes policies to permit public sector pay to rise without adequate restraint – as seems to have happened in Britain in 1979–80 – is an example of political prejudice (or prior commitments) leading to misguided macroeconomic policies. A government can always adopt a public sector pay policy that will make matters worse (that is, cause more wage inflation than would otherwise have occurred) – whether or not it can usefully exercise considerable downward pressure on the *general* level of wage settlements. The adoption of a sensible mix of macroeconomic policies should therefore not be thought of as a substitute for a sensible and responsible pay policy in the public sector; indeed, the latter is one aspect of a macro policy that takes due account of the especially marked price-increasing effects of certain types of government outlays.

Attempts to exert more direct influence over private sector price and wage settlements (including policies operated through tax incentives) may or may not be feasible in particular countries and particular circumstances; and they may or may not lead to subsequent reactions when the controls are relaxed. But the likelihood of their succeeding depends largely upon whether appropriate macroeconomic policies are being adopted at the same time; for, if this is not so, a relaxation of the incomes policy (which is likely to occur eventually) will lead to rapid wage and salary increases. In the same way, if the country's macroeconomic policies are well chosen, there is also likely to be less need to attempt to apply extensive prices and incomes policies. The demand for incomes policies usually arises either when a government has allowed the general level of demand to rise too high, or when the pursuit of monetary policies that (temporarily) hold down real post-tax interest rates, coupled with high tax rates, has led to inflation at less than full employment. The appropriate remedy is clearly to cut taxes and sell attractive bonds until full employment without inflation is restored. If some sort of prices and incomes policy (perhaps in the form of a temporary 'freeze') can speed the movement from high to low inflation this may well be helpful; but if appropriate combinations of macroeconomic measures are applied, such prices and incomes policies should become unnecessary before long – and they will be unworkable if the mix is ill-chosen.

Indeed, the mix of low real post-tax interest rates and high levels of taxation in the 1970s and early 1980s presumably made it harder to restrain money-wage increases. Not only did high tax rates on wage and salary earners tend to raise their wage and salary demands (at any given level of employment), but the mix did nothing to make employers less ready to accede to these demands. For the higher are tax rates on profits, the greater the proportion of any rise in the wage and salary bill that may be thought of as being 'paid by the government' (as being a tax-deductible business expense); and the lower are real post-tax rates of interest, the less the effective cost of borrowing if some non-taxable benefit, such as freedom from strikes, is thereby obtained.

Wage demands and temporary reductions in inflation

Suppose a change in the policy mix reduces the rise in the price level for a limited period, but after that prices continue to rise as they would have done without the switch of mix. Can there be any reasonable doubt that the switch of mix will have some effect on wage bargaining during the period of the switch of mix?[3]

During the period of the switch there is no doubt that the rate of inflation that is occurring will be less, and that so far as this has any effect on wage bargains, it will tend to reduce wage settlements during that period. The rate of change in real post-tax income (for any given real pre-tax income) will certainly have been increased for that period, and post-tax income will be correspondingly higher at each future period, unless taxes had to be higher in future to a fully offsetting extent (and if the original switch of mix had no lasting helpful effect). Even if we cannot be sure how far a temporary success in reducing the upward march of prices will affect wage bargains, it would in principle be worth having for other reasons; and it could only increase the probable success of any other measures to restrain money-wage increases.

OBSTACLES TO A SOUND MIX

The political obstacles that stand in the way of tax cuts and tight monetary policies seem to have been extraordinarily powerful in the recent past – especially when one bears in mind the great political benefits available to the community as a whole if the adoption of appropriate forms of mix had enabled the economy to operate at a higher level of activity without any greater upward pressure on prices. It is therefore important to identify the principal political obstacles.

One powerful obstacle to the adoption of a less inflationary mix is the opposition of the business world – which is consistently a net borrower – to paying high, or at least positive, real-interest rates, after a decade or more in which borrowers have often been able to borrow at low or negative real post-tax interest rates. It is true that high *nominal* rates of interest probably act as a deterrent to investment; but the right remedy for this situation is to cut taxes without easing monetary policy – for easing monetary policy would continue to hold up rates of inflation, and so nominal interest rates, whilst also continuing to deprive lenders of a positive real return on their lending. Yet the business sector as a whole would clearly benefit greatly from the adoption of policies that would check inflation whilst making possible a return to full employment. It is thus in the interests of business generally to advocate low taxation and a return to positive real post-tax returns to lenders, coupled with expansionary policies applied by means of an anti-inflationary mix.

The obsession of the business world in many countries with the avoidance of budget deficits seems to spring from pre-occupation with the *financing* of the deficit. If the government has to borrow more, the business world feels, there will be less for private business to borrow. But this is only part of the story; for the tax cuts or government spending that cause the budget deficit also make possible higher incomes for business; and if the adoption of lower tax rates and the issue of honest bonds makes possible less deflationary policies there will be both less need for business to borrow (as tax payments will be lower) and also more funds for it to borrow (as incomes generally will then be higher). Obsession with holding down the budget deficit (as

118 Unemployment, Inflation and New Macroeconomic Policy

distinct from the desirable aims of according proper attention to financing it in non-inflationary ways, and to ensuring that the forms of taxation and government outlays are appropriate) has thus led to dangerously stagflationary policies, which are not likely to be reversed until the business world understands the damage that the policies that t has been supporting have been doing to the world economy.

Yet when businessmen are asked whether they would prefer to have lower taxes (or higher subsidies) rather than lower interest rates, most would opt for the former; and surely all of them would opt for a switch of mix in that direction if it was coupled with a higher level of real activity and less inflation. Again, in the long run everyone would benefit by overcoming this political obstacle; but attention is always focused unduly on individual elements in the mix, in this case the fear of (temporarily) higher nominal interest rates.

In contrast to the trading companies of the business world – which are net borrowers – financial institutions are of course, in general, neither net borrowers nor net lenders. But they often oppose increases in nominal interest rates, as being likely to reduce the capital value of their assets, and this often leads them to support excessively expansionary monetary policies. Yet such policies eventually lead to still higher nominal interest rates, whereas tighter monetary policies coupled with tax cuts would hold down both inflation and nominal interest rates, taking one year with another. On the other hand, the banks benefit from having many of their liabilities fixed in money terms (or bearing very low nominal interest), so that as nominal interest rates rise on their lending, they stand to reap large profits. In any case, like everyone else, the financial world stands to gain from a cessation of stagflation. If the financial world supported more enlightened policies for restoring a high rate of growth with an anti-inflationary mix, it would be much more likely that such policies would be adopted. As it is at present, however, the financial world seems often to ally itself with the rest of the business world in demanding deflationary policies applied by way of what are inflationary mixes of macroeconomic measures.

The household sector, in contrast to the business sector, is a net lender. In their capacity as households, therefore, the public have interest in the restoration of positive real post-tax returns to the lender; and they clearly have also a strong interest in the restoration of high employment without serious inflation. Yet the political influence that is wielded by the lobby of those with mortgages on their houses seems often to stand in the way of the adoption of monetary and tax policies that would benefit everyone in the longer run. But even current mortgage borrowers stand to gain more from the restoration of full employment with lower rates of inflation (and eventually lower nominal interest rates) than they can lose from any temporary rise in nominal interest rates; and future house-owners will benefit from the consequently lower prices they would pay for housing if returns on financial assets became higher in real terms.

Perhaps the most serious obstacle lies right at the seat of economic power – in treasuries (and to some extent in central banks). For treasuries have evolved historically as guardians of the public purse, and this has given them a strong built-in assumption (which colours almost all their thinking) that one of their main tasks is to safeguard the public revenue and to keep down the burden of the national debt. This leads them to view with equanimity the rise in revenue that usually results (under progressive tax systems) from inflation, and also the fall in the real burden of the national debt that occurs in inflationary periods. They are similarly averse to cuts in tax rates (sometimes being known to say that once one reduces them it may be difficult to persuade politicians to raise them again), and to measures that raise the level of interest payments that has to be financed. They, and central bank advisers, are notoriously sceptical about the possibility of persuading the public to buy any particular volume of bonds: but (as a defence, or at least an excuse, for their attitude) it must be said that they have the continual problem of finding markets for the bonds; and that the tacit underlying assumption they are usually making is that politicians will resist putting up the return on bonds to levels that the public will find attractive (an assumption that is usually justifiable). In this sense, at least, it might be fairer to place the blame on the politicians than on their advisers; and fairer still to place it on the electorate at large – including economists – for not urging politicians to place as much weight on the interests of the public in their capacity of lenders as on that of the public as borrowers.

A serious obstacle to the reduction of those forms of government spending that are excessive is the generally well organised opposition of those groups that benefit from each individual spending programme, including those who are employed in implementing the programmes. The *cost* to the community of using resources for any particular form of government spending – rather than for some other purpose (whether in the private or public sector) where it would be put to better use is not represented by any such lobby; so that minorities can usually muster political support for particular outlays from which their members benefit. The same may be said of those forms of tax concession that benefit particular groups or industries. When tax concessions are made in particular directions, or subsidies given to assist particular activities or particular firms or industries, this makes it correspondingly more difficult to make the general tax cuts that are needed to reduce the general level of costs in the economy: and tax cuts or subsidies that merely benefit particular industries can be (and have been) misrepresented by the governments providing them as being a means of assisting industry *generally* – whereas what is required is a general reduction in the taxes imposed on all businesses, together with an *elimination* of *differential* forms of assistance (whether by subsidies, tax concessions, tariffs, import controls or other means) that favour *particular* industries or products. The public interest is for a change of policy away from differential assistance and towards general tax cuts. A powerful lobby for such a policy would be invaluable. If it were to be formed, perhaps consumer associations, journalists and economists would be the most likely nucleus for organising it.

Another vested interest of crucial importance is that of economists and financial journalists who have still not properly adapted their ways of thinking to handling the dual problem of stagflation; and are therefore still apt to pursue the long-established habit of one-dimensional thinking, which almost invariably considers only the consequences of a *single* policy change (rather than a change in *combinations* of measures) and its effects on one objective (inflation *or* the level of employment) at a time (rather than both inflation and unemployment together). The strongest vested interest of all is that of established ideas. But the arguments being advanced in this book do not imply a need to throw overboard the accumulated intellectual capital of the past four or five decades, but merely to complement it with additional dimensions. This being so, it remains difficult to understand the built-in resistance there seems to be to discussing the rather obvious question: 'What *combinations* of measures will do most to solve the *dual* problem of stagflation?' rather than the questions 'What should we do to reduce unemployment?' or 'What should we do to stop inflation?' Yet neither the 'monetarist' approach nor the 'anti-monetarist' or 'Keynesian' contains sufficient dimensions for dealing with situations where there are both inflation and unemployment. An appropriate modification of our ways of thinking about macroeconomic issues generally, by adopting a framework for discussing the relative effects on alternative objectives of different instruments, is thus of the utmost urgency.

THE MIX AND RECENT MACROECONOMIC CONTROVERSIES

It may be useful to place the proposals that have been advanced in the present book in the context of recent controversies between the so-called 'monetarists' and 'anti-monetarists' or 'Keynesians' (even though a large measure of agreement seems to have been reached of late among the more moderate adherents of each of these schools of thought, at least at a theoretical level).

The discussion of the mix merely adds additional dimensions to ways of thinking about macroeconomic policy. In effect, it takes the view that governments that follow *either* monetarist *or* Keynesian policy prescriptions have as good a chance of being wrong as of being right, as the crucial element of the proper choice of instruments is generally missing both when a monetarist tells a government to control the quantity of money and when a Keynesian tells it to raise or reduce the level of aggregate demand. Neither the Keynesian nor the monetarist approach tells governments about the considerations that determine the relative effects upon prices and output (respectively) of alternative ways of bringing about a given change in aggregate demand (for a Keynesian) or the quantity of money (for a monetarist). Yet this is the crucial question for an economy in a state of stagflation. By contrast, the monetarist assumes, implicitly or explicitly, that the economy is at full employment or that it will tend to return there; and that changes in the quantity of money affect only prices in the longer run; whereas the Keynesian tends to assume that the particular combination of measures with which a given stimulus to aggregate demand is provided does not make any difference to the price effect for any given rise in employment. Whether one's approach is basically Keynesian or basically monetarist, therefore, it needs to be combined with due consideration of the relative effects on prices and employment of the alternative macroeconomic instruments; and, if this essential extension of the basic ways of thinking about the issues is made, it is perfectly feasible for either a basically monetarist or a basically Keynesian approach to be combined with proper attention to the policy mix.

The 'monetarist revival' drew much needed attention to the failure to take due account of the rapid rise in the quantity of money that had resulted from easy money mixes. But the consequence has been that monetary targets have become aims in themselves – even when this aim has been achieved by the use of mixes that made stagflation worse, and when disproportionate attention to that monetary target has diverted attention from seeking the best combination of measures to stop stagflation.

THE DANGERS OF NOT ADOPTING THE WHOLE MIX

Economists have often been faced by the problem that, when they suggest a package of measures, politicians have adopted those elements in it that seem electorally attractive, whilst omitting equally essential elements with which they disagree, or which they feel likely to be electorally unpopular. This sort of 'selectivity' can, and usually will, result in making matters worse economically. This is especially liable to occur with proposals for the combinations of measures that have been suggested in this book. For one element – but not the other – in any one of the two-pronged packages that have been suggested (as broad aggregative illustrations of the principles for policies that could stop stagflation) is likely to be electorally attractive whereas the other is not.

The mix of tax cuts and tight monetary policy is obviously likely to be attractive to politicians (or at least to their electors) on the *budget* front, but they may fear the adverse electoral consequences of keeping *monetary* policy tight (even though a sufficiently long perspective of the post-war period ought by now to have convinced even the most sceptical of them that the use of monetary measures to hold down interest rates results eventually in more inflation and therefore higher nominal interest rates). In the long run, therefore, this – the best policy mix for solving the problem of stagflation – may well bring special political gains for a party espousing it, at least after a brief period, when nominal interest rates may, indeed, go up.

The mix of reducing government spending and taxation (as a proportion of total output) is again obviously likely to be popular with politicians (and with those who elect them) on the tax side. Restraints on government spending (in general, and in the abstract) may also win them some votes. But reductions in any particular form of government spending naturally elicit strong opposition from those most adversely affected by them, and are therefore difficult to carry out. The risk is therefore that this half of that particular mix may not be properly implemented and that governments will consequently feel unable to reduce taxes either, and so will perpetuate the stagflation. But, conversely, there is also the risk that conservative-minded governments may succeed in checking the government spending, but not reduce taxes far enough or fast enough to prevent this from causing a rise in unemployment.

In a third type of mix, the rise in *government spending* will usually be electorally popular – especially with governments on the left of politics; whereas the necessary other element of keeping *monetary policy* very tight is likely to be highly unacceptable to them. The chances are, therefore, that a government of the left will increase government spending, but not keep monetary policy tight enough – and that it might increase types of government spending that would make inflation much worse.

In all, therefore, it is not surprising that many governments have adopted policies, especially tax cuts, that can be represented (though incorrectly) as moving in some degree towards one of the mixes that has been advocated above, when the politically attractive element in the package has *not* been complemented by an appropriate setting of the other instrument, or instruments, to achieve the reduction in stagflation. In *this* sense, indeed, there are no painless solutions: for *some element* in any solution will be politically unattractive. But much of the 'pain' that has to be suffered is essentially for the politicians and those who discuss their policies, in that they have to change many of their cherished assumptions as to what is desirable, or what is electorally feasible, if adequate solutions to macroeconomic problems are to be found.

Most of the analysis in earlier chapters has been made, for simplicity, in terms of considering only two macroeconomic instruments at a time. But in reality, of course, all the macroeconomic instruments have to be used simultaneously. It may be appropriate, therefore, to look at all three groups of instruments together, and to stress the importance of adopting also the politically awkward element (or elements) in any package at the same time as that which is most likely to win votes.

If the level of government spending is relatively high, either taxation must be kept relatively high or else monetary policy must be tighter, in order to establish a given level of employment. If the aim is to stop stagflation, it has been argued above that it is best to keep monetary policy tight – even though politicians seem often (probably, quite wrongly) to regard this as politically more unattractive than keeping taxes high.

The lower is the level of taxation, the lower must government spending be, or else the tighter must be monetary policy (again, in order to establish any given level of employment). There is no general presumption as to which of the last two will be best for holding down the price level at a given level of taxation; it depends largely on the type of government spending under consideration. But both present obvious political difficulties – with no general presumption as to which will be the greater political liability.

Finally, the easier is monetary policy, the higher must be taxation or the lower must be government spending – obviously both alternatives being politically awkward. But high tax rates are likely to hold up prices at any given level of employment, whereas cuts in government spending are more likely to reduce prices (unless they are of types that reduce costs by more than alternative uses of the same resources could).

THE MIX AT FULL EMPLOYMENT

The discussion of the policy mix in earlier chapters was in the context of a situation of stagflation, where the choice of a less inflationary mix could be taken as likely to make a government willing to operate the economy at nearer to full employment than would have occurred if it was trying to use high unemployment as a restraint on inflation. Clearly, the social and economic gains from adopting an anti-inflationary mix are greatest in this situation, because of the additional output and employment that result from the choice of an appropriate mix for minimising inflation with a lower level of unemployment over the period in question.

When full employment is restored, however, the gains from adopting an anti-inflationary mix are clearly less – as in that situation no reduction in unemployment will result from adopting a less inflationary mix. But it will still be true that a mix that gives rise to less upward pressure on prices at the given level of employment will generally be preferable, and will certainly reduce the risk that governments will feel inclined at some future date to resort to unemployment in the hope that it will be a cure for inflation.

The same basic principles that underlie the choice of an appropriate policy mix in a situation of stagflation can be applied also at full employment. For, at full employment also, a mix with a very rapid rise in the quantity of money – brought about by an expansionary setting of monetary policy – will cause more inflation than will one with lower tax rates and a tighter monetary policy. In nominal terms, the former mix would give rise to a greater risk (or a greater amount) of excess demand than the latter. Indeed, the analysis has in the past often been made in terms of a so-called 'inflationary gap', resulting from an excess of total demand (in nominal terms) over available supplies at the prices prevailing at the start of the period. In real terms, however, demand cannot be greater than available supplies at genuinely full employment. One can therefore equally well describe this as 'excess demand' or as 'the choice of an inflationary mix' at full employment.

If the least inflationary mix is chosen to restrain inflation, this will almost certainly involve allowing nominal interest rates to be temporarily high, or at least refraining from trying to hold them down by monetary measures. But as the choice of a tight monetary mix will minimise the upward pressure on prices, it will in the longer run also hold down nominal interest rates. By contrast, if a government that is worried about inflation at or near full employment adopts the wrong combination of anti-inflationary measures to reduce excess demand, it may cause unnecessary unemployment in the process of trying to reduce inflation; for too little of the effect will then be on prices and too much on employment. In the past, governments have often in fact tried to cure excess demand inflation by undue reliance upon tax increases, whilst making insufficient, or belated, use of a tighter monetary policy. This has meant that more unemployment has had to be created to achieve a given reduction in inflation than would have been necessary with

Criticisms, Complications and Conclusions 125

the opposite mix. Indeed, by a sufficiently skilful use of tight monetary policy, combined with sufficiently low tax rates, it should be possible to remove excess demand without creating unemployment.

By contrast, the tendency in many countries during the 1950s and 1960s, and especially in the late 1960s and the 1970s, was for governments to raise taxes in booms and then not reduce them to a fully offsetting extent in recessions; whereas even when they did – often belatedly and inadequately – allow monetary policy to be tightened in booms (though sometimes still leaving real post-tax interest rates lower than they had been in situations of higher unemployment) they took the first opportunity to reduce interest rates (rather than taxes) when the boom seemed to have passed. This meant that over the decades of the 1950s and 1960s there was a sort of 'ratchet' effect, with tax rates generally rising and real post-tax interest rates falling from one cycle to the next. This may go far to explain the drift into stagflation in the 1970s.

This is not to discount the relevance of the orthodox analysis of rising marginal costs in an economy near to full employment. For that merely says that the *real* cost of producing another unit of output rises sharply as full employment is approached. Taken by itself, this is certainly a factor tending to raise the price level. But the extent to which this *real*-cost factor will raise the *nominal* price level depends upon monetary factors. If the quantity of money and tax rates were held down sufficiently in the face of the approach of full employment, more aggregate output could be squeezed out of the economy without so much inflation (for any rise in real costs) than if monetary policy had been more expansionary and tax policy correspondingly tighter.

THE MIX AND THE OVERALL SETTING OF DEMAND

This book has been concerned mainly with the differential advantages and disadvantages of the various macroeconomic instruments, from the viewpoint of their respective effects on the price level and on the level of real output of employment. But macroeconomic policy is concerned not only with obtaining the best combination of instruments to achieve a particular level of employment, but also with achieving the right level of employment.

In other words, the standard analysis that concentrates on achieving 'full employment' (on some appropriate definition) is no less important than it has been in the past. Indeed, it comes into its own again once it is appreciated that there is no unique 'trade-off' (in any sense) between employment and inflation that might have made it seem necessary to prejudice that objective.

The overall setting of macroeconomic policy ought thus to be such as to restore or maintain full employment, and the combination of measures chosen for that purpose ought to be the least inflationary one available. Thus, if we start from a situation of stagflation, the overall setting of policy needs to be such that unemployment will be reduced – provided that this is done in a way that reduces inflation (rather than one that increases it). In particular, this is likely to involve a reduction in tax rates, and in tax revenue *at any given* level of output; but not necessarily in actual tax revenue, nor necessarily a rise in the actual budget deficit – which will tend to fall as full employment is restored. Starting from high unemployment, monetary policy naturally ought not to be tightened sufficiently to offset all the stimulus that would normally be the result of the cuts in tax rates.

If, however, the economy is at or near full employment, the overall setting of policy in real terms would need to be kept more or less constant; so that any tax cuts that were undertaken with a view to reducing cost-inflation from that source would need to have their expansionary impact offset fully by tighter monetary measures. Similarly, if a reduction in government outlays (as a *ratio* of total output) were the complementary measure to the tax cuts, at full employment this would, indeed, involve a reduction in the real *level* of government outlays, whereas in a situation of stagflation it could well be consistent with an actual rise in government spending.

A government should be seeking to vary all the available instruments together, in such a way as to achieve the best results. At or near full employment, a tax cut made with a view to checking cost-inflation would thus necessitate *either* cuts in government outlays *or* a tightening of monetary policy; and the greater the use made of one of these complements, the less the use that would need to be made of the other. By contrast, starting from a situation of stagflation, a given tax cut would not have to be accompanied by so great a tightening of monetary policy, or such a large reduction in the share of government outlays to total output, as would be needed at or near full employment; for the net effect of the measures when there was substantial unemployment (in real terms) would need to be stimulatory. It would still be true, however, that the greater the tightening of monetary policy the less would be the need for cuts in the ratio of government to total spending (and vice versa).

At a more disaggregated level, so far as it is possible to generalise about the relative effects on prices and output of sub-groups of these main instruments, variations within each of these groups may be made with the same end in view. At the present time, however, the presumption must be that we do not know enough to say with confidence very much about which taxes and government outlays have the greatest cost-inflationary effects –

Criticisms, Complications and Conclusions 127

though we may reasonably expect that a cut in indirect-tax rates will have some immediate downward effect on costs and prices, whereas cuts in direct-tax rates may have their cost-reducing effects over a longer period. We should certainly not rush to change the relative importance of various taxes in the tax structure (at least on macroeconomic grounds) without a careful investigation of their relative effects on the price level. Morover, if their relative role in the tax structure is changed for non-macroeconomic reasons, it should be only after attention has been paid also to the repercussions of such changes upon the possibility of achieving macroeconomic objectives.

CONCLUSION

The proposals in this book are consistent with restraining the rate of increase in money incomes, or the rise in the volume of money, which is one feature of the policies being widely applied in the early 1980s. But the argument of the preceding chapters is that this approach needs complementing by giving due attention to the particular combination of tax rates, government spending and monetary policy with which any given rise in nominal incomes, or of the quantity of money, is achieved. For if it is achieved with relatively high tax rates (and high levels of many forms of government spending), coupled with low or even negative real post-tax returns to lenders, the upshot is likely to be continued high inflation and high unemployment – as it was with this combination of measures in the later 1970s.

At the same time, the policies often advocated by critics of current policies – higher government spending and easier money (and perhaps higher tax rates) – would probably be as bad in the longer run as are current policies, for they would raise inflation more than employment. A steady rate of increase in nominal demand (for which a steady rate of increase in the quantity of money may or may not be a good approximation) could be a helpful element in a satisfactory solution – but only if it is achieved by way of very much lower tax rates (and with reductions in the most inflationary forms of governments spending) coupled with a return to the issuing on an adequate scale of honest bonds yielding a sufficient and predictably positive real post-tax return to lenders.

In short, the discussion of this book has been mainly about achieving the right *balance* among the main groups of instruments. At least half of our attention in macroeconomic policy discussions ought in future to be devoted to considering these matters of the balance, or mix, of instruments. This balance, or 'ensemble', of the instruments is as important as the *overall* effect that is being achieved on employment by the setting of the instruments at any given time. If due attention is paid to it in future, macroeconomic policy could once again achieve the high degree of success that was usual in the 1950s and 1960s.

Notes and References

CHAPTER 1: INTRODUCTION AND SUMMARY

1. Some theorists use the term 'rate of inflation' to mean 'the sustained underlying rate of inflation'. But in the real world it is normally used to mean the rate of increase in the price level over some particular period; and that is the concern of policy makers in practice. In any case, it is impossible in fact to tell whether or not any particular rise in the price level will or will not be continued; so that the only usage that makes sense in the discussion of real policy issues is the generally accepted one. (See R. G. Lipsey, 1979, p. 285.)
2. The real rate of interest is positive if the nominal yield on the asset in question exceeds the actual (or, in some formulations, the expected) rate of inflation. Where the lender pays tax on the interest, the real return from the asset is not positive unless the pre-tax interest rate exceeds the product of the rate of inflation and the tax rate; and the pre-tax return must rise faster than any rise in the tax rate, in order to maintain any given real post-tax yield. (See pp. 32–4.)
3. An algebraic exposition of the basic proposals is to be found in Perkins (1979, Appendix 2); and there is a geometric exposition of them in Perkins (1980) and in Jones and Perkins (1981, Chapters 25 and 26).

CHAPTER 2: CURRENT MACROECONOMIC PROBLEMS AND POLICIES

1. Recorded figures understate the rise in the number of people without work, as many people who would have liked to have a job did not continue to seek one in the depressed conditions of the 1970s. On the other hand, a partly offsetting factor was that many women who in earlier decades would not have been part of the officially registered work force were now registered as unemployed.
2. Attempts have sometimes been made to obtain a so-called 'discomfort index', or 'index of macroeconomic misery' by adding together indicators for inflation and unemployment. (See, for example, OECD [McCracken], 1977, p. 42.) The addition of two such incommensurable quantities makes no economic sense, especially in periods over which they move in opposite directions – though it is understandable that people should seek some combined indicator of macroeconomic policy success or failure. If one knew what weight governments assigned to given changes in each of these indicators one could make some attempt to compile a relevant type of index. But, as it happens, the deterioration in *both* inflation *and* unemployment between the 1960s and 1970s was so clear

cut that there is no need to try to compile any such combined indicator in order to make broad comparisons between these two periods. It is possible also to compare the macroeconomic performance of the mid-1970s with that of the late 1970s (or even the early 1980s, so far as data are available) without the need to weight the two indicators; for *both* unemployment *and* inflation were higher in 1980 than they were in 1975 or on the average of the years 1974-6. It is therefore clear that the macroeconomic policies pursued since the mid-1970s did not result in any improvement in macroeconomic performance over that period.
3. This indicator understates the cost-inflationary effects when there is a heavy reliance on direct taxation and widespread avoidance and evasion of it, as this probably exerts strong upward pressure on wage and salary demands by those subject to tax-deduction at the source.
4. See, for example, Friedman (1968).
5. Unpublished lecture to Erasmus Society, cited in Wilson (1980).
6. I am grateful to Bob Jones for having convinced me of the importance of not referring to 'the supply of money' when one means 'the quantity of money actually in existence'.

CHAPTER 3: THE BASIC PROPOSALS

1. See Corden (1981) and Corden and Dixon (1980).
2. Lindbeck has described this effect in Lindbeck (1980, p 17). He points out that the effect in question is likely to be particularly large in situations where the short-term supply elasticities are small for the relevant asset goods. But it would surely be more exact to say that supply elasticities *must* be low if this effect is to lead to a general rise in costs − for otherwise a shift of demand in the opposite direction would have just as much effect on costs. The crucial consideration is thus that people usually choose to move towards these goods largely *because* they are in rather inelastic supply; yet they must also be goods whose prices affect those of newly produced substitutes (*new* houses, *new* gold output etc.).
3. See Parkin (1980).
4. See Bacon and Eltis (1976).
5. This section owes much to discussions with Ivor Pearce.

CHAPTER 4: BALANCE OF PAYMENTS ASPECTS

1. Articles bearing on the policy mix in an open economy are Dernburg (1974); Argy and Salop (1979); and Bilson (1979).
2. I have benefited greatly from discussions with David Vines on the issues discussed in this section.
3. The policy suggestions made in this section are consistent with the diagnosis, though not fully consistent with the prescriptions, contained in the stimulating analysis of Britain's economic problems in Gould, Mills and Stewart (1981). These writers suggest that the current policies that hold down economic activity in Britain and reduce her international competitiveness are the opposite of what is required. But their prescription includes the use of a very expansionary monetary policy to stimulate British industry, and over-emphasises the extent of

Notes and References 131

the need for devaluation as a means of improving the competitiveness of British industry. But, surely, the more the competitiveness of British industry can be improved, instead, by the use of a less inflationary mix, the better: and so far as devaluation is a necessary part of the policy, the less the extent to which it is brought about by expansionary *monetary* measures, the better. Yet the prescription of these writers seems likely to increase unnecessarily the upward pressure on prices associated with any given real stimulus and with any given improvement in Britain's international competitiveness. By contrast, it is probable that a stimulus brought about with a relatively tight monetary policy and correspondingly larger tax cuts (as suggested in the present text) would eventually do more to reduce nominal interest rates than would the easing of monetary policy recommended by Gould, Mills and Stewart. For it is policies that are directed towards easing monetary measures that are most likely to raise nominal interest rates in any but the very short-run.

The easing of monetary policy, coupled with tax increases, in Britain in February and March 1981 contributed to the sharp depreciation of ensuing months (and consequent upward pressure on prices). The tightening of monetary policy later in the year constituted an implicit acknowledgement, and partial reversal, of the mistakes made earlier in the year.

CHAPTER 5: THE MIX, THE BUDGET AND THE NATIONAL DEBT

1. Income-tax indexation is discussed more fully, in the context of the role of various types of indexation in dealing with stagflation, in Jones and Perkins (1981, Chapter 27).
2. My interest in these issues was stimulated by Jim Pemberton (Pemberton, 1980). The section on these issues in this chapter benefited greatly from his comments on an earlier draft and from discussions with him.
3. See Taylor and Threadgold (1979); Bank of England (1979); and Siegel (1979). This section has benefited from discussions of these issues with Andrew Threadgold and Chris Taylor.

CHAPTER 7: CRITICISMS, COMPLICATIONS AND CONCLUSIONS

1. See Pitchford and Turnovsky (1976); and Rowthorn (1977).
2. The so-called 'real-wage overhang' has been discussed by the OECD in various issues of *Economic Outlook* during the period 1978–80.
3. This doubt appears to exist in the mind of at least one writer. See Pemberton (1980).

Bibliography

Argy, V. and Salop, J., 'Price and Output Effects of Monetary and Fiscal Policy under Flexible Exchange Rates', *IMF Staff Papers* (June 1979).

Auld, D. A. L., 'The Impact of Taxes on Wages and Prices', *National Tax Journal* (March 1974).

Auld, D. A. L. and Brennan, G., 'The Tax Cut as an Anti-Inflationary Measure', *Economic Record* (December 1968).

Australian Economic Review (1: 1979), Symposium on Macroeconomic Policy.

Bacon, R. and Eltis, W., *Britain's Economic Problem: Too Few Producers* (London: Macmillan, 1976).

Bank of England Quarterly Bulletin (December 1979), 'The National Debt: A Supplementary Note'.

Bilson, J. F. O., 'The Vicious Circle Hypothesis', *IMF Staff Papers* (March 1979).

Blinder, Alan S., 'Can Tax Increases be Inflationary?', *National Tax Journal* (June 1963).

Corden, W. M. 'Taxation, Wage Rigidity and Unemployment', *Economic Journal* (June 1981).

Corden, W. M. and Dixon, P. B., 'A Tax-wage Bargain for Australia: Is a Free Lunch Possible?' *Economic Record* (September 1980).

Dernburg, Thomas F., 'The Macroeconomic Implications of Wage Retaliation Against Higher Taxation', *IMF Staff Papers* (November 1974).

———, 'Indexing the Individual Income Tax for Inflation: Will This Help Stabilise the Economy?', U. S. Congress (December 1976).

Friedman, Milton, 'The Role of Monetary Policy', *American Economic Review* (June 1968).

Gordon, R. J., 'Inflation in Recession and Recovery', *Brookings Papers in Economic Activity* (No. 1, 1971).

Gould, B., Mills, J. and Stewart, S., *Monetarism or Prosperity?* (London: Macmillan, 1981).

Jones, R. S. and Perkins, J. O. N., *Contemporary Macroeconomics* (Melbourne: Prentice-Hall, 1981).

Lindbeck, A., *Inflation: Global, International and National Aspects*, (Leuven: University Press, 1980).
Lipsey, R. G., 'World Inflation', *Economic Record* (December 1979).
OECD, *Towards Full Employment and Price Stability*, 'McCracken' Report (June 1977).
Okun, Arthur M., 'An Efficient Disinflationary Policy', *American Economic Review (Papers and Proceedings)* (May 1978).
Parkin, Michael, 'Oil-push Inflation?' *Banca Nazionale del Lavoro Quarterly Review* (June 1980).
Pemberton, J. A., review of *The Macroeconomic Mix to Stop Stagflation*, *Economic Journal* (September 1980).
Perkins, J. O. N., *The Macroeconomic Mix to Stop Stagflation* (London: Macmillan, 1979).
———, 'Using the Macroeconomic Mix to Stop Stagflation', *Journal of Economic Studies* (1: 1980).
———, 'Macroeconomic Policy and Economic Growth', in Irma Adelman (ed.), *National and International Policies*, Vol. 4 of *Economic Growth and Resources*: Proceedings of the Fifth Congress of the International Economic Association (London: Macmillan, 1979).
Pitchford, J. D. and Turnovsky, S. J., 'Income Distribution and Taxes in an Inflationary Context', *Economica* (August 1975), and 'Some Effects of Taxes on Inflation', *Quarterly Journal of Economics* (November 1976).
Rowthorn, R. E., 'Conflict, Inflation and Money', *Cambridge Journal of Economics* (no. 3, 1977).
Siegel, Jeremy, J., 'Inflation-induced Distortions in Government and Private Savings Statistics', *Review of Economics and Statistics* (February 1979).
Stephens, J. Kirker, *Inflation, Unemployment and the Macroeconomic Policy Mix* Centre for Economic and Management Research (University of Oklahoma, 1980).
———, 'An Empirical Note on Some Monetarist Propositions: Comment', *Southern Economic Journal* (April 1980).
———, 'The Current State of the Selectivist Alternative to Keynesian and Monetarist Macropolicy', *Journal of Economics* (1980).
Taylor, C. T. and Threadgold, A. R. ' "Real" National Saving and its Composition', *Bank of England Discussion Paper* no. 6 (October 1979).
Thorn, Richard A., review of *The Macroeconomic Mix to Stop Stagflation*, *Journal of Money, Credit and Banking* (June 1980).
Wilson, Thomas, 'Robertson, Money and Monetarism', *Journal of Economic Literature* (December 1980).

Index

Argy, V., 130
Australia
  and CAP, 101
  policy in resources boom, 61–2
Austria, 24, 35
avoidance, tax, 27–9

Bacon, R., 130
balance of payments
  and macroeconomic policy, 53–67
  as aim of policy, 10
Bank of England, 131
'beggar-my-neighbour' policies, 63–6
Bilson, J. F. O., 130
Britain
  and oil, 58, 61–2
  balance of payments, 61–2, 65–6
  bank borrowing, 19
  indexed bonds, 36–7
  interest rates, 19, 56, 65–6
  policy, 21, 38, 43
  PSBR, 10, 23, 68, 73–4, 85
  stagflation, 65–6
  'U-turn', 21
budget deficit
  and capital inflow, 73–4
  and government spending, 70–4, 76, 78–89
  and national debt, 78–89
  as aim of policy, 10, 23, 110, 117–18
  as indicator, 17, 23, 68–71
  as target, 10–11, 68–87
  in recession, 10, 71–2
  'real', 82–9
  unimportant, 68–71
budgetary policy
  and deficit, 68–76, 78–89
  and monetary policy, 16–17, 44, 49–51, 122–5
  and national debt, 78–89
  and quantity of money, 39, 76
  in closed economy, 6–9, 21, 23–30, 36, 40–52, 68–89, 109–11, 117–18, 122–7
  in open economy, 53–60, 63–7

CAP, see EEC, Common Agricultural policy
Canada
  and CAP, 101
  policy, 43
capital flows, and macroeconomic policy, 53–60, 64–7
Corden, W. M., 130

debt, national
  and inflation, 78–89
  policy, 78–89
deficit, see budget deficit
developing countries
  and protection, 2
  and stagflation, 2
  exports, 1
Dixon, P. B., 130

EEC, Common Agricultural Policy (CAP), 28, 99, 101
Eltis, Walter, 130
evasion, tax, 27–8
'evoison', 27–8
exchange-rates
  and inflation, 53–67
  and resource allocation, 60–6
  as target, 10
exhaustible resources, and interest, 36–9

Finland, 43

Index

Friedman, Milton, 130
full employment, policy mix, 123–5

Germany, West, policy, 24, 35, 38, 56, 65–6
Gould, B., 131
government spending, 23–5, 40–1, 48–52, 68–76, 119–20, 122
  and deficit, 72–6
  and private sector, 72–3
  in open economy, 53–60
  growth, and stagflation, 3–4

import controls, and inflation, 90–1
indexation
  of financial assets, 36–7
  of income tax, 76–8
inflation
  and bank borrowing, 18–19
  and expectations, 111–13
  and government spending, 40–1, 41–2
  and interest, 15, 26–40
  and resource allocation, 95–7
  and saving, 83–4
  and tax rates, 23–30, 108–9
  and unemployment, 1, 5, 15, 23, 38, 109–13
interest rates
  and bank lending, 19
  and exhaustible resources, 36–9
  and inflation, 15, 30–40
  and resource allocation, 10, 96–8
  and taxation, 32–9
  and wages, 116
  as cost, 47
  as indicator, 17
  as target, 10–11
  in 1970s, 6–10, 37–8
  in open economy, 53–60, 63–7
  policy, 53–60, 63–7
  political considerations, 117–19
  real, 1–2, 6–9, 18–19, 30–40
investment
  and policy mix, 95–9
  and prices, 98
Ireland, 43

Japan, 38, 65–6

Jones, R. S., 129, 130

Keynesians, and mix, 50, 120–1

Lindbeck, Assar, 130
Lipsey, R. G., 129

McCracken, P., 129
macroeconomic policy, *see* budget deficit, budgetary policy, exchange-rates, monetary policy, open economy, resource allocation policy, resources boom, targets, taxation
Mills, J., 131
monetarism, and macroeconomic mix, 50, 120–1
monetary policy, 16–19, 23–5, 30–40, 47–8, 49–50, 110–11, 116, 122–7
  and balance of payments, 23–4
  and interest rates, 17
  and quantity of money, 10–11, 16–19, 39
  in open economy, 53–60, 63–7
money, demand, 17–19

national debt, 78–89
New Zealand, and CAP, 101

OECD
  bond rates, 6, 8–9, 35
  government spending, 6
  inflation, 5–7
  policy, 11–12, 20–2, 24, 35
  taxation, 6–7, 9
  unemployment, 5–7
objectives, macroeconomic, 10–13
obstacles, to sound mix, 117–20
oil, price rises, 5, 37–9
open economy, macroeconomic policy, 53–67
overdrafts, and taxation, 18–19

Parkin, Michael, 130
Pearce, Ivor, 130
Pemberton, J. A., 131
Perkins, J. O. N., 54, 129

Index

productivity
  and taxation, 35, 45-7, 60-1
  and interest rates, 35, 96-9, 109
  and unemployment, 3, 93-5, 105
protection
  and developing countries, 2, 99
  and inflation, 2-3, 10, 90-3
  and income distribution, 2
  and stagflation, 2, 10, 90-3
  and unemployment, 2, 10, 90-3

Reagan, policies, 21
resource allocation policy
  and exchange rate policy, 60-3
  and interest rates, 96-9, 109
  and inflation, 90-107
  and macroeconomic policy, 2, 10, 90-107
  and stagflation, 2, 90-107
  and unemployment, 2, 10, 90-107
resources boom, and macroeconomic policy, 61-3
Robertson, Dennis, 15

Salop, J., 130
saving
  and inflation, 83-4
  'real', 83-4
Seigel, Jeremy, J., 131
stagflation, *see* Britain, inflation, protection, resource allocation policy, unemployment
Stewart, S., 131
Switzerland, 24, 35

targets, macroeconomic, 10-13, 16-18, 121
tariffs, 90-3
taxation
  and bank borrowing, 18-19
  and inflation, 1-2, 5-10, 26-30, 45-7, 108-13
  and interest rates, 32-7
  and national debt, 78-89
  and production, 35, 45-7, 60-1
  and quantity of money, 16, 39
  and resource allocation, 95-8, 109
  and wages, 113-17
  as cost, 26-30, 45-7, 60-1, 108-9
  company, 29
  excise, 28
  expenditure, 28
  in 1970s, 6-10
  in open economy, 53-60, 63-7
  income, 29, 76-8
  indexation, 76-8
  payroll, 28, 61
  policy, 23-30, 32-6, 43-52, 110-13, 122-7
  sales, 28
Taylor, C. T., 131
technological change, and unemployment, 3-4, 101-5
Threadgold, A. R., 131
transfer payments, 74-6

unemployment
  and growth, 93-5
  and inflation, 1-2, 5-15, 23, 38, 109-13
  and national debt, 83-9
  and production, 105
  and productivity, 3, 90-2, 93-5
  and protection, 2, 90-3
  and resource allocation, 90-5
  make-work 'remedies', 101-5
  temporary or permanent?, 20
United States
  and CAP, 101
  and 'supply-side' effects, 26-7
  policy, 21, 27, 65-6
'U-turn', 21-2

Vines, David, 130

Wages
  and inflation, 38, 113-17
  and taxation, 26, 28-9, 46, 113-17
Wilson, Thomas, 130

GPSR Compliance
The European Union's (EU) General Product Safety Regulation (GPSR) is a set of rules that requires consumer products to be safe and our obligations to ensure this.

If you have any concerns about our products, you can contact us on

ProductSafety@springernature.com

In case Publisher is established outside the EU, the EU authorized representative is:

Springer Nature Customer Service Center GmbH
Europaplatz 3
69115 Heidelberg, Germany

www.ingramcontent.com/pod-product-compliance
Ingram Content Group UK Ltd.
Pitfield, Milton Keynes, MK11 3LW, UK
UKHW041419180426
11947UKWH00007B/206